GOVERNMENT RESPONSES TO THE LATIN AMERICAN DEBT PROBLEM

Edited by

Robert Grosse

North·South Center Press
UNIVERSITY OF MIAMI

The mission of the North-South Center is to promote better relations and serve as a catalyst for change among the United States, Canada, and the nations of Latin America and the Caribbean by advancing knowledge and understanding of the major political, social, economic, and cultural issues affecting the nations and peoples of the Western Hemisphere.

To order or to return books, contact Lynne Rienner Publishers, Inc. at 1800 30th Street, Suite 314, Boulder, CO 80301-1026, 303-444-6684, fax 303-444-0824

Library of Congress Cataloging-in-Publication Data

Government responses to the Latin American debt problem / edited by Robert Grosse.
    p. cm.
    At head of title: North-South Center, University of Miami.
    Includes bibliographical references and index.
    ISBN 0-935501-96-7 (alk. paper)
    1. Debt relief—Latin America. 2. Debts, External—Latin America.
    I. Grosse, Robert E. II. University of Miami. North-South Center.
HJ8514.5.G68 1995   95-18232
336.3'435'098—dc20   CIP

Printed in the United States of America

00 99 98 97 96 95 6 5 4 3 2 1

GOVERNMENT RESPONSES TO THE LATIN AMERICAN DEBT PROBLEM

CONTENTS

CONTRIBUTORS

Diego Aramburú is an economic consultant in Miami, Florida. He works for several financial institutions designing and managing portfolios of Latin American securities. He has written several articles about Latin American external debt and about the secondary market in government external debt.

Humberto Campodónico is professor of international economics at San Marcos University and also professor of economic development at the National Engineering University, both in Lima, Peru. He also serves as a principal investigator in the research firm DESCO in Lima. He recently wrote the book *Macroeconomic Policies and Power Elites in Peru* (DESCO 1994).

Jaime Delgadillo is an economic consultant in Miami, Florida. He served as general manager and member of the Board of Directors of the Banco Central de Bolivia and as chief negotiator of the external debt during the late 1980s. He was also professor of international economics and techniques of international negotiations at Universidad Católica Boliviana.

Sergio Fadl graduated from the Instituto Tecnológico Autónomo de México (ITAM). He is currently assistant to the director general of the Banco Nacional de Comercio Exterior (BANCOMEXT). From 1989 to 1992, he participated in the restructuring of Mexico's external debt. He has written numerous articles about external debt, reform of the Mexican financial system, swaps, and other financial topics.

Robert Grosse is chairman of the World Business Department at the American Graduate School of International Management in Glendale, Arizona. He is also director of the Thunderbird Business Research Center. Professor Grosse has worked extensively in Latin America and is the editor of the North-South Center book, *Private Sector Solutions to the Latin American Debt Problem* (1992).

José Angel Gurría did graduate studies at the University of Leeds (England), the University of Southern California, and Harvard University. He is currently secretary of external affairs of Mexico. From 1982 to 1993, he was lead negotiator of the public sector to restructure external debt for Mexico. He has written many articles about external debt, capital flight, and other macro financial topics.

Erik Haindl is director of the Institute of Economics at the Universidad Gabriela Mistral in Santiago, Chile. He is also professor of international economics and economic development at the University. He was formerly the director of the Institute of Economics at the Universidad de Chile. He is a member of the panel of fiscal experts of the International Monetary Fund.

Evan Tanner is associate professor of economics at the University of Miami in Coral Gables, Florida. During the 1994-1995 academic year, he served as a Fulbright Scholar in Argentina and Brazil.

Carlos von Doellinger holds an M.A. degree from Universidade Federal de Rio de Janeiro. He is currently professor of economics at the Universidade Candido Mendes in Rio de Janeiro, Brazil.

I

INTRODUCTION AND OVERVIEW

Robert Grosse

RATIONALE

The Latin American debt crisis has been examined from numerous perspectives over the past decade. From its origins in the 1970s (e.g., Kuczynski 1987; Marichal 1989) — to its nature as a liquidity or solvency crisis (e.g., Cline 1983; Grosse 1988) — to the financial instruments and institutions that have been created to deal with it (e.g., Frenkel, Dooley, and Wickham 1989; Krugman 1989; Errunza and Moreau 1989; Aramburú and Grosse 1991) — to its relationship with Latin American economic development (e.g., Sachs 1988; Twentieth Century Fund 1992) — the literature has treated and continues to analyze many of the critical issues involved.

An area of relative disregard has been the reaction of Latin American governments to the external debt problem since the mid-1980s. That is, the process of economic opening, as well as broader fiscal and monetary policy reform, has resulted in a range of government strategies for dealing with the remaining large public sector debt "overhang." With over $250 billion of foreign commercial bank debt still owed by Latin American official borrowers in 1994, the problem is far from solved. Government policies, such as the reduction of trade barriers and the privatization of state-owned companies, have been discussed widely. The overall foreign debt strategies of these countries have been explored much less in the literature. The fundamental purpose of this project is to put these government responses into clear focus and to compare and contrast them among Latin American countries in the early 1990s.

This kind of analysis is especially important in the context of restarting the process of sustained economic growth in the region. Even though positive growth in national income has occurred in most Latin American countries

1

since 1989, the growth paths have diverged widely in different countries, and the government strategies likewise differ quite markedly among countries. Are the Brady Plans in countries such as Mexico and Venezuela really contributing in an important way to those economies? How has the dramatic shift in overall economic policy in Mexico been linked to the external debt problem? What direction is Brazil currently following, and where can that country be expected to head in the next few years? And finally, what is the U.S. government's perspective on the debt situation as it has developed? These questions illustrate some of the focal points of the papers that constitute this project.

ANTECEDENTS

The *Government Responses* project follows a series of analyses concerning *Private Sector Solutions to the Latin American Debt Problem* that were carried out by the North-South Center in 1991 (Grosse 1992). Those analyses demonstrated the critical inputs of the lending banks, foreign and domestic investors, and other private sector participants that helped to defuse the crisis nature of the debt problem. From the development of the secondary market in Latin American loans to the use of debt-equity swaps and country funds, these private sector firms have played a central role in the debt resolution process. By the same token, the borrowing governments also played key roles in the same process, both as partners with the lenders and as overseers and regulators of the economies where new investments are taking place today. Thus, this focus on the government responses is a logical second step in the North-South Center's debt program.

The authors who participated in this *Government Responses* project carried out most of the research for their papers in 1992 and 1993. They met in a conference at the University of Miami in January 1994 to present their papers and to participate in a discussion of the debt experiences across the region. The conference was sponsored jointly by the North-South Center and Hamilton Bank. Formal comments on the papers were presented during the conference, and selected comments are included here following two country chapters.

OVERVIEW OF FINDINGS

Each of the first five authors examined a particular country's experience in dealing with the external debt over the past several years. Erik Haindl looked at the Chilean case, a clear success story by the early 1990s. He finds that Chile followed a classic macroeconomic policy, once the debt crisis had taken hold. That is, Chile's government in the early 1980s faced a large current account deficit, an external debt that by 1984 exceeded the value of its gross domestic product (GDP), and very high debt interest payments stemming from high dollar interest rates in the international market. In response, the government implemented greater economic opening; conservative fiscal measures, which produced a budget surplus in several years and reduced the government's foreign borrowing from 1984 onward; and a stable monetary policy, with inflation of about 20 percent per year during the decade.

Haindl argues that Chile's success in dealing with the external debt problem was due principally to the export-led growth policy, though it must also be seen as depending on the reduction in government sector debt and on successful monetary stabilization. By using a policy of undervaluing the currency, the government was able to stimulate exports and discourage imports. In addition, Chile established arguably the most successful program for swapping external debt for equity investment and other local uses. This program alone was able to reduce Chile's external debt by about $11 billion from 1985 to 1991. According to Haindl, "The end result was not only a solution to the external debt problem, but a healthier and more competitive economy."

A contrasting story is portrayed by Carlos von Doellinger who examines the case of Brazil. The Brazilian experience during the past decade has been characterized by very high inflation and a persistent inability to resolve the external debt problem. The successive governments of military and then elected leaders have been unable to cut public spending and monetary growth sufficiently to escape bouts of hyperinflation. At the same time, Brazilian policy toward the external debt has been relatively confrontational, characterized by a series of renegotiations with official multilateral and bilateral lenders as well as with commercial bank lenders, punctuated by a unilateral moratorium on payments to commercial banks during 1987-1988.

Beginning in 1986, Brazilian governments have imposed five major stabilization plans to control inflation and deal with government spending and revenue inadequacies, as well as with misaligned interest rates and inflationary expectations. In all cases, the plans have failed to correct the inflationary spiral. As far as the foreign debt is concerned, this problem has been consistently relegated to a lesser position of importance in policymaking as compared to domestic economic conditions. As in other countries of the Latin American region, Brazil has repeatedly renegotiated external debt in the three categories (multilateral, bilateral, and commercial). Thus far, the final solution to this problem is not clear. Perhaps Brazil will negotiate a Brady Plan package of debt restructuring that will indeed finally eliminate the recurrent bouts of renegotiations on the commercial bank debt. Perhaps the economic growth process will generate enough confidence in the country to stimulate capital inflows sufficient to defuse the shortages of foreign exchange that characterized the 1980s.

The Brazilian case is quite interesting because, despite the seemingly overwhelming problems of hyperinflation and fiscal imbalance, the country has achieved economic growth rates among the best in the world during the early 1990s. Although the government has failed to come to grips with the fundamental macroeconomic issues of the day, the economy is growing exceptionally well at this point. Apparently, it is possible to achieve an acceptable growth path without achieving the macroeconomic stability that is generally acknowledged to be a necessary precondition. This assertion is obviously subject to debate and to empirical verification as Brazil moves through the 1990s.

Evan Tanner comments on the Chilean and Brazilian papers, focusing mainly on the issue of whether or not the debt strategies had an important impact on the country's economic growth path. He questions the value of Chile's debt-equity swap program, since the resources used in this program could arguably have been used more efficiently elsewhere in the economy. He likewise questions the significance of Brazil's inability to deal with the debt, while the country nevertheless has produced impressive economic growth. Despite these warnings about the unclear links between debt and growth, Tanner ends with a statement of concern for Brazil's economy, linked to the unresolved problems in domestic macroeconomic policy.

A case intermediate between those of Chile and Brazil is presented by Humberto Campodónico, who examined the Peruvian experience. Campodónico found that during the 1980s, the Peruvian governments were essentially unable to cope with the external and internal economic crises, neither under Fernando Belaunde's relatively conservative administration nor under Alan García's populist leadership. It remained for a nontraditional leader, Alberto Fujimori, to establish a policy framework and implement steps to cope with external debt and internal stagnation, along with terrorism and enormous social strife.

Peru suffered enormous economic setbacks during the 1980s, with per capita income falling throughout most of the decade. The external debt was only one of many severe problems, not the least of which was the fact that more than one-half of the economy was estimated to operate in the underground (informal) sector. The alternating orthodox (1980-1985) and leftist (1985-1990) economic policies made essentially no difference in dealing with the public sector external debt, which went unpaid beginning in 1983.

It was only with the election of President Fujimori in 1990 that Peru's government really undertook a strategy for resolving the external debt problem. Thus, Campodónico's paper focuses on this most recent period. The government negotiated a debt restructuring agreement with the International Monetary Fund (IMF) and another with the Paris Club of lender governments that allowed the crisis to be resolved and a path to debt management established. Concomitant with the debt restructuring, and as a requirement of the IMF financing, Peru was required to follow orthodox monetary and fiscal policy reforms that were indeed put into place. Inflation dropped from more than 10,000 percent per year in 1989 to under 100 percent per year in 1991.

In sum, the Fujimori government negotiated new credit terms and implemented major policy reforms that put the country on a path to deal successfully with the external debt problem.

The story is not so simple, however. Complications such as the *autogolpe* of 1992, in which Fujimori took dictatorial control of the country and disbanded Congress, added new complexity to the picture, since official lenders were strongly against supporting nonelected governments. The capture of the country's main terrorist leader in 1992 gave a major boost to confidence in the government and improved social conditions significantly. Return of flight capital aided in local investment, but at the same time caused the currency to revalue, making exports less competitive in world markets. In sum, the package of reforms since 1990 has created a dramatically improved position for the economy, although per capita income still has not grown much into the mid-1990s.

The lessons to draw from the Peruvian experience are rather complex, due to the concurrence of several major crises. One conclusion by Campodónico is that the debt problem has not really been resolved, since significant increases in debt servicing needs will come due in the next two to three years. Debt reduction along Bolivian lines (see below) has not been adequate to escape the cycle thus far. Fortunately, as of 1994, investor confidence in the country remains high, and so financial resources are not lacking for private sector development at this time. Campodónico warns of the lack of investment in social services, which, coupled with slow per capita income growth, leaves a potential social problem untended. The public sector external debt situation seems to be manageable if private sector financial resources continue to flow into the country during the rest of the decade.

A much clearer success story in the Andean region comes from Bolivia, which was examined by Jaime Delgadillo. The Bolivian economic crisis showed many parallels with that of Peru in the early 1980s: a relatively low-income country, a balance of payments crisis with massive capital outflows, runaway inflation, a large fiscal deficit, and a huge portion of the economy operating in the informal sector. Bolivia's government responded directly to the crisis much earlier than Peru's did, with the resulting economic shock and recovery occurring much sooner.

In 1985, Bolivia's government undertook a dramatic program of economic restructuring, which included the renegotiation of external debt with commercial bank lenders, with foreign governments, and with multilateral lending agencies (mainly the IMF, World Bank, and Inter-American Development Bank). The debt restructurings were not ultimately completed for several years, as Bolivia sought and received greater extensions on its repayment periods and reduced interest rates, as well as some reduction of principal repayments.

The most striking feature of the Bolivian debt resolution was the treatment of commercial bank debt. This debt constituted about one-third of the total external debt in 1985. As a result of the government's offer to repurchase this debt at 11 percent of face value, with funds donated by foreign governments, Bolivia was able to eliminate most of its debt in 1987. This plan, plus some conversion of the remaining debt into local uses (e.g., debt-equity swaps and debt donations for environmental projects) reduced the commercial bank debt to only 7 percent of total external debt in 1991. The crisis was clearly over at that point.

From 1986 to 1992, debt from official sources was renegotiated several times through the Paris Club for the bilateral government loans and through direct negotiations with the IMF and other multilateral lenders. Bilateral debt within the Latin American region was directly canceled through accords with the governments of Argentina and Brazil. The net result is that today more than 90 percent of Bolivia's sovereign external debt is with official lenders, in which maturities are quite long (greater than ten years), interest rates are quite favorable, and grace periods often exist before amortization of principal.

Bolivia has not escaped the problems of being a small, less-developed country, but it has put itself on a solid footing for sustained growth into the next century by dealing successfully with both domestic and external macroeconomic crises of the 1980s.

The final country case study was carried out by José Angel Gurría and Sergio Fadl, who looked at the experience of Mexico during and since the external debt crisis. The Mexican case is especially interesting because Mexico was the country whose external debt problem crystalized the crisis in 1982. When the Mexican government declared its inability to meet interest payments on foreign commercial bank debt in August 1982, the world took clear note of the crisis nature of less-developed country (LDC) external debt. Within months, other countries in Latin America and elsewhere made similar declarations. The resulting LDC debt crisis was characterized by high interest burdens, a reduced ability to generate export surpluses due to commodity price declines, and subsequent reschedulings, renegotiations, and eventual debt reductions that have appeared in all the country case studies.

As the two largest debtors, Mexico and Brazil shared much of the spotlight in this period. While Brazil's external debt problem has yet to be resolved, Mexico offers a much happier outcome. Nevertheless, the process of achieving the positive results that Mexico has obtained was costly and tortuous. During the early and mid-1980s, Mexico's GDP did not grow at all; and for the entire decade, per capita income actually fell. The early response to the debt crisis was to cut spending and money supply growth, which, along with the drastic cutback in foreign financial resources due largely to high dollar interest rates and low petroleum prices, produced a severe recession.

The macroeconomic situation improved in Mexico as early as 1984, with positive income growth and a trade balance surplus.

However, the initial improvement in Mexico's economic situation was reversed by a renewed sharp decline in oil prices and revenues in 1986. Once again, the country was unable to generate adequate foreign exchange to meet debt servicing commitments, and again renegotiation of the debt was required. At this stage, the government demonstrated a strong commitment to dealing with the crisis through economic growth and restructuring of the debt. Mexico joined the General Agreement on Tariffs and Trade (GATT) in 1986 and opened the economy significantly to international competition. Mexico became one of the first countries (after Chile) to embrace the use of debt-equity swaps in 1987, allowing foreign investors to buy Mexican sovereign debt in the secondary market and exchange it for capital investment in the country. And Mexico carried out additional steps to reduce, rather than just reschedule, the foreign debt, such as the program to convert debt to long-term bonds backed by U.S. Treasury zero-coupon bonds that was launched in 1988. This program retired more than $3 billion of foreign debt in exchange for $1.1 billion of new long-term bonds.

Perhaps more than anything else, Mexico's government demonstrated a flexibility in dealing with the external debt problem: New mechanisms were frequently utilized to reduce the debt burden. Mexico was the first country to reach a Brady Plan accord in 1990; this agreement led to the restructuring of $48 billion of commercial bank debt through bond swaps and new money commitments. One of the terms in the bond agreements was for Mexico's interest payments to be adjusted up or down if the price of oil were to move up or down relative to the $14 per barrel price in 1989. In addition, Mexico permitted debt donations to nonprofit users in the country for purposes of education and environmental protection, among others. This eliminated almost $1 billion of debt, which was converted into peso funding of social projects. The range of tools created and used to reduce the debt burden was very broad and ultimately very effective in meeting that task.

Gurría and Fadl conclude that Mexico has escaped the overindebtedness problem. The primary steps that achieved this result are the successful programs to restructure the debt and the domestic macroeconomic policies that coped with inflation and reduced the government's fiscal deficit. All of these steps helped to restore investor confidence in the Mexican economy, leading to a willingness of both foreign and domestic investors to place their funds into Mexican investments. The need to maintain investor confidence is seen as a critical requirement for continuing the process of sustained economic growth and controlling inflation.

Moving from the country-specific analyses, the book concludes with two studies of the regional situation, comparing country experiences. The first study focuses on the Brady Plans that have been negotiated with five Latin American countries and explores the relative success of each country in reducing the debt burden through its Brady Plan. The second study looks at the creditworthiness of ten countries in the region and considers the factors that have enabled some countries to achieve better results than others in the eyes of international private sector lenders.

The Brady Plan was launched by U.S. Treasury Secretary Nicholas Brady in 1987 as a mechanism for dealing with the LDC external debt crisis and the concomitant problem of large amounts of nonperforming debts on the books of several large U.S. international banks. The plan essentially took the range of solutions that had been initiated by commercial bank lenders during the mid-1980s and formalized a process through which government borrowers in the LDCs could offer their creditors a portfolio of alternatives for restructuring the debt. The portfolio generally consisted of alternatives such as exchanging loans for long-term bonds with reduced principal amounts, buying back debt at or near the secondary market price, and converting loans into new bonds with reduced interest rates.

Diego Aramburú compared the financing terms of the five Brady Plan experiences in Latin America: those of Mexico, Costa Rica, Venezuela, Uruguay, and Argentina. His analysis describes the details of the financing alternatives offered and used in each of the five plans. He found that the commercial bank lenders who participated in these restructurings opted most often for collateralized par bonds as the conversion mechanism to return their loans to performing assets. This mechanism calls for replacement of existing loans with new long-term bonds that offer below-market interest rates, extended maturities, and guarantees of principal repayment through the use of U.S. Treasury zero-coupon bonds held to cover repayment. Par bonds accounted for 48 percent of the rescheduled sovereign commercial bank debt.

The second most common alternative selected for restructuring the sovereign commercial bank debt in Brady Plans was the discount bond. Under this arrangement, the lender converted nonperforming loans into long-term bonds carrying competitive interest rates, but the principal value was reduced from the original face value, effectively reducing the value of the outstanding debt. Discount bonds accounted for about one-third of the total Brady Plan restructuring in the five Latin American cases.

The remaining alternatives used by commercial banks in restructuring their Latin American loans through Brady Plans were noncollateralized par bonds and direct buy-back of the debt at a discount. This last choice produced a direct reduction in the debt and servicing requirements, though, of course, it required the delivery of cash to carry out the repurchase. These two types of conversion accounted for the remaining 20 percent of the debt that was restructured in the Brady Plans. For Latin America as a whole, the Brady Plans produced the restructuring of approximately $90 billion of the total commercial bank debt of $290 billion or of the total external debt of $450 billion.

These experiences constituted major responses to the debt crises that were burdening each of the countries involved. While some countries, such as Bolivia and Chile, were able to escape the debt crisis before the Brady Plan initiative, the majority of governments in the region have either taken advantage of the plan or are in the process of doing so. Whether the Brady Plan restructurings and economic policy reforms will enable these countries to return to a state of sustained economic growth remains to be demonstrated. The plans themselves formed one clear and significant step toward that end.

The final paper in the project, by Robert Grosse, considered the Latin American governments' successes in dealing with the external debt as evidenced by their return to international creditworthiness. In this case, the measurements of success were a credit rating or a price of the government's debt in the international market. All the governments in the region have improved their international creditworthiness since the trough of the debt crisis in 1987. Nevertheless, some of them, such as Chile and Colombia, have achieved notable successes in bringing their foreign debt up to essentially fully competitive status in the world financial markets. Others, such as Ecuador and Peru, remain mired in significant debt problems.

Grosse's analysis posited fundamental economic and policy factors that would be expected to affect international lenders' perceptions of the creditworthiness of Latin American sovereign borrowers. He found that conditions in the international economy — namely, dollar interest rates and the rate of growth of the industrial countries — affected the creditworthiness of the Latin American countries more than any other factors. These factors are obviously beyond the control of the borrower countries.

In addition, significant influences on creditworthiness were found from the level of international reserves to total external debt and (negatively) from the size of the government budget deficit. Interestingly, the greater the proportion of long-term debt to short-term debt in the country's portfolio, the better its creditworthiness. Apparently, the government's ability to obtain long-term credit commitments has translated into greater perceived creditworthiness.

These last two studies complement the country case studies by exploring the relative successes of different governments in achieving solutions to the external debt crisis. Aramburú's study limited itself to just those five countries that have negotiated Brady Plans and compared the outcomes of those negotiations. Grosse's study considered both Brady Plan countries and others in the region, comparing the secondary market prices of their sovereign commercial bank debt and the probabilities of repayment of that debt.

REFERENCES

Aramburú, Diego, and Robert Grosse. 1992. "The Secondary Market in Latin American Loans." In *Recent Developments in International Banking and Finance,* ed. Sarkhic Khoury. Cambridge, Mass.: Blackwell.

Cline, William. 1983. *International Debt and the Stability of the World Economy.* Washington, D.C.: Institute for International Economics.

Errunza, Vihang, and John Moreau. 1989. "Debt-for-Equity Swaps under a Rational Expectations Equilibrium," *Journal of Finance,* July.

Frenkel, Jacob, Michael Dooley, and Peter Wickham. 1989. *Analytical Issues in Debt.* Washington, D.C.: International Monetary Fund.

Grosse, Robert. 1988. "Resolving Latin America's Transfer Problem," *The World Economy,* September.

Grosse, Robert, ed. 1992. *Private Sector Solutions to the Latin American Debt Problem.* Coral Gables, Fla.: University of Miami North-South Center.

Krugman, Paul. 1989. "Market-Based Solutions to the Latin American Debt Problem." Paper presented at the American Enterprise conference on LDC debt, March 19, Washington, D.C.

Kuczynski, Pedro-Pablo. 1987. "The Outlook for Latin American Debt," *Foreign Affairs,* Fall.

Marichal, Carlos. 1989. *A Century of Debt Crises in Latin America.* Princeton, N.J.: Princeton University Press.

Sachs, Jeffrey. 1988. "The Debt Overhang of Developing Countries." In *Debt, Growth, and Stabilization,* ed. Ronald Findlay. Oxford: Blackwell.

Twentieth Century Fund. 1992. *In the Shadow of the Debt.* New York: Twentieth Century Fund.

II

CHILE'S RESOLUTION OF THE EXTERNAL DEBT PROBLEM

Erik Haindl

ORIGINS OF THE EXTERNAL DEBT PROBLEM

One of the biggest problems that faced the Chilean economy in the 1980s was the external debt problem. In a short period of time, a booming economy that had reached an average growth rate of 8.1 percent in the period from 1976 to 1981 entered into a deep recession in 1982-1983. Chile became an overindebted country almost overnight, and the huge capital inflows stopped at the same time that Mexico had problems in servicing its external debt. Most of the economic crisis that followed is closely related to this situation.

The external debt problem influenced all macroeconomic policy in Chile from 1981 onward. Chile's policy was oriented principally toward solving the overindebtedness and returning to a normal situation. The effort was successful, and by the beginning of the 1990s, Chile was again growing at an average rate of 6 percent per year, and the external debt problem was solved. Since the Chilean experience is a success story, it is interesting to examine the origins of the external debt problem and the government's response to this problem.

By the second half of the 1970s, Chile was pursuing a complete opening of the economy and free market policies in most areas. Average tariffs went down from about 90 percent to a uniform 10 percent rate, and the existing multiple exchange rates were merged into one. Most of the enterprises in state hands were privatized, and the size of the public sector was reduced significantly. A profound fiscal reform introduced the value added tax as the main revenue raiser, changed the progressive personal income tax, and reduced public expenditure, turning a fiscal deficit into a surplus. In addition, the inflation rate was reduced from 508 percent per year in 1973 to 31 percent in 1980 (see Table 1).

Table 1
Chile: Macroeconomic Indicators 1976-1980
(in percentage)

	1976	1977	1978	1979	1980
GDP growth	3.5	9.9	8.2	8.3	7.9
Inflation(CPI)	174.3	63.5	30.3	38.9	31.2
Unemployment	12.7	11.8	14.2	13.6	10.4
Fiscal deficit as % of GDP(-)	1.4	-1.1	-0.1	4.8	5.4
Ext.debt/GDP	53.1	42.0	45.5	41.8	40.6

Source: Central Bank of Chile.

Several factors have been suggested as an explanation for the creation of an external debt problem in Chile. Some of these factors are internal and refer to Chilean economic policy, and others are external, related to the international environment. The fact that almost all Latin American countries entered into a similar debt crisis, while they were pursuing quite different economic policies, suggests that the external factors played a key role. Internal policies served only to alleviate or to exacerbate the problem, but are certainly not the principal cause of it.

The main external factor explaining the large capital inflows to Chile was the abundance of international private bank lending, caused by huge deposits made by the oil exporting countries and the low real interest rate for international lending. As soon as Chile started to open its capital account in 1977, the economy received a growing capital inflow, which induced a high current account deficit. The current account started with a surplus of 1.5 percent of GDP in 1976 and ended with a deficit equal to 14.5 percent of GDP in 1981 (see Table 2).

This growing current account deficit induced a high growth in aggregate expenditure (absorption), which produced a downward pressure on the real exchange rate. The fall in the real exchange rate generated a "boom" in the non-tradable sector (see Table 3). Profits in the non-tradable sector made investments in this area very attractive, so that most of the international lending was used to finance projects in that sector. Real wages went up, especially in 1980 and 1981, and Chilean workers received for the first time high salaries in dollar terms, even by international standards.

In 1981, the Chilean economy experienced a sharp deterioration in terms of trade and a rise in the real interest rate paid on foreign debt. Average export prices fell by 13.4 percent in 1981 and by a further 16.5 percent in 1982 (see Table 5). This meant a loss of revenue equivalent to 3.3 percent of 1980 GDP. Almost all of this loss was financed by new credits, through an increased current account deficit (see Table 2).

Table 2
Chile: Current Account, 1976–1984
(millions US$)

	1976	1977	1978	1979	1980	1981	1982	1983	1984
Goods:									
-Exports (FOB)	2,116	2,186	2,460	3,835	4,705	3,836	3,706	3,831	3,651
-Imports (FOB)	(1,473)	(2,151)	(2,886)	(4,190)	(5,469)	(6,513)	(3,643)	(2,845)	(3,288)
Trade balance	643	35	(426)	(355)	(764)	(2,677)	63	986	363
Services:									
-Exports	297	417	481	785	1,263	1,172	936	797	664
-Imports	(507)	(720)	(735)	(1,027)	(1,554)	(1,741)	(1,377)	(1,204)	(1,181)
Invisible trade	(210)	(303)	(254)	(242)	(291)	(569)	(441)	(407)	(517)
Income (net):									
-Direct investment	(4)	(23)	(88)	(85)	(82)	(121)	(128)	(136)	(179)
-Interest	(322)	(342)	(401)	(590)	(848)	(1,342)	(1,793)	(1,612)	(1,845)
-Other	(7)	(14)	(16)	(22)	(99)	(132)	(114)	(45)	(40)
Total income payment	(333)	(379)	(505)	(697)	(1,029)	(1,595)	(2,035)	(1,793)	(2,064)
Unrequited transfers	48	96	97	105	113	108	109	97	107
Total current account	148	(551)	(1,088)	(1,189)	(1,971)	(4,733)	(2,304)	(1,117)	(2,111)
Current account as a percentage of GDP	1.5%	-4.1%	-7.1%	-5.7%	-7.1%	-14.5%	-9.5%	-5.7%	-11.0%

Sources: Central Bank; IMF.
FOB = Free on Board.

Table 2, cont.
Chile: Current Account, 1985-1993
(millions US$)

	1985	1986	1987	1988	1989	1990	1991	1992	1993
Goods:									
-Exports (FOB)	3,804	4,191	5,223	7,052	8,080	8,310	8,929	9,986	9,202
-Imports (FOB)	(2,920)	(3,099)	(3,994)	(4,833)	(6,502)	(7,037)	(7,353)	(9,237)	(10,180)
Trade balance	884	1,092	1,229	2,219	1,578	1,273	1,576	749	(978)
Services:									
-Exports	692	1,042	1,085	1,214	1,536	1,999	2,260	2,540	2,580
-Imports	(1,057)	(1,480)	(1,506)	(1,808)	(2,114)	(2,215)	(2,191)	(2,405)	(2,413)
Invisible trade	(365)	(438)	(421)	(594)	(578)	(216)	69	135	167
Income (net):									
-Direct investment	(156)	(171)	(214)	(303)	(382)	(333)	(643)	(1,132)	(956)
-Interest	(1,888)	(1,721)	(1,486)	(1,616)	(1,543)	(1,478)	(1,166)	(727)	(702)
-Other	(35)	(39)	(42)	(50)	(57)	(43)	(33)	(36)	(30)
Total income payment	(2,079)	(1,931)	(1,742)	(1,969)	(1,982)	(1,854)	(1,842)	(1,895)	(1,688)
Unrequited transfers	147	85	126	177	215	199	340	431	425
Total current account	(1,413)	(1,192)	(808)	(167)	(767)	(598)	143	(580)	(2,074)
Current account as a percentage of GDP	-8.6%	-6.7%	-3.9%	-0.7%	-2.7%	-2.0%	0.4%	-1.4%	-4.7%

Sources: Central Bank; IMF.

Table 3
Chile: Absorption and "Boom" in Non-tradable Sector
(in percentage)

% change in	1977	1978	1979	1980	1981
Absorption	14.2	9.7	10.5	9.4	12.3
Real exch. rate	-13.9	1.2	-9.5	-7.5	-3.4
Real wages	6.3	2.0	1.0	13.8	15.4
Tradable GDP	7.8	4.5	7.0	5.5	3.8
Non-tradable GDP	11.3	10.7	9.1	9.5	7.6

Source: Central Bank of Chile.

The rise in the real interest rate paid on foreign debt was a direct consequence of former President Ronald Reagan's economic policy, which applied a contractionary monetary policy in the context of a high fiscal deficit. LIBOR (London Interbank Offered Rate) and prime interest rates went up, and U.S. inflation went down, increasing the real interest rate paid on foreign debt dramatically (see Table 4). Real interest rates paid on foreign debt were negative in the second half of the 1970s and turned positive in the 1980s. In 1980, the average real interest rate paid on foreign debt was 1 percent and rose to 7.7 percent in 1981 and to a record high of 10.4 percent in 1982.

Table 4
Chile: Real Interest Rate Paid on Foreign Debt
(percentage)

	1976-1979	1980	1981	1982	1983
LIBOR	8.6	14.2	16.7	13.4	9.9
Prime rate	8.9	15.5	18.8	14.7	10.8
Avg. int. paid	7.9	13.3	17.3	14.7	10.5
US inflation CPI	8.5	12.3	8.9	3.9	3.7
Real int. paid	-0.6	1.0	7.7	10.4	6.6

Sources: IMF; Central Bank of Chile.

Since most of the foreign debt was defined in terms of floating interest rates, tied either to LIBOR or prime, there was an automatic rise in Chilean foreign net factor payments. This situation contributed to a further deterioration in the current account and is the single main cause of the external debt problem. In fact, using the real interest rate paid in 1980 as a reference, net factor payments of 1981 were 41 percent higher than otherwise (which represents a loss equivalent to 1.4 percent of GDP), and net factor payments of 1982 were 83 percent higher (with a net loss equivalent to 4.6 percent of GDP). Had real interest rates stayed constant at historical levels, Chile probably would never have entered into an external debt problem.

Table 5
Chile: Export and Import Performance, 1976–1984
(percent change)

	1976	1977	1978	1979	1980	1981	1982	1983	1984
Exports:									
- Quantum	24.4%	11.9%	11.2%	14.1%	14.3%	-3.4%	13.7%	5.4%	-0.1%
- Price	7.0%	-7.7%	1.2%	36.6%	7.3%	-13.4%	-16.5%	-1.9%	-4.5%
- Value	33.1%	3.3%	12.5%	55.9%	22.6%	-16.3%	-5.1%	3.4%	-4.6%
Imports:									
- Quantum	4.3%	35.5%	17.6%	22.7%	18.7%	21.0%	-36.8%	-13.5%	15.6%
- Price	-7.1%	7.7%	14.1%	18.4%	9.9%	2.7%	-12.3%	-9.8%	0.2%
- Value	-3.1%	45.9%	34.2%	45.3%	30.5%	24.3%	-44.6%	-22.0%	15.8%
Terms of trade index	136.10	116.63	103.45	119.37	116.56	98.31	93.58	101.72	96.91
Purchasing power of exports index	59.33	56.88	56.10	73.88	82.46	67.15	72.68	83.28	79.29

Sources: 1976-1980 National Accounts;
1981-1992 Central Bank.

Table 5, cont.
Chile: Export and Import Performance, 1985–1992
(percent change)

	1985	1986	1987	1988	1989	1990	1991	1992
Exports:								
- Quantum	13.4%	7.7%	5.4%	7.4%	11.5%	11.5%	7.0%	14.2%
- Price	-7.8%	2.5%	14.6%	28.6%	4.2%	-6.1%	-1.4%	-2.0%
- Value	4.6%	10.4%	20.8%	38.1%	16.2%	4.7%	5.5%	11.9%
Imports:								
- Quantum	-13.4%	15.2%	18.4%	17.5%	29.3%	3.2%	7.1%	28.3%
- Price	-0.7%	-7.8%	9.9%	6.2%	6.2%	4.8%	-0.9%	-1.1%
- Value	-14.0%	6.2%	30.1%	24.8%	37.3%	8.2%	6.1%	26.9%
Terms of trade index	89.97	100.00	104.29	126.41	124.69	111.78	111.15	110.09
Purchasing power of exports index	83.50	100.00	109.95	143.07	157.36	157.29	167.33	189.30

Sources: 1976-1980 National Accounts;
1981-1992 Central Bank.

Table 6
Chile: External Debt, 1976-1984
(millions US$)

	1976	1977	1978	1979	1980	1981	1982	1983	1984
Public sector:									
-Central bank (1)	1,030	953	1,135	1,276	1,070	577	843	2,983	4,454
-Treasury	1,615	1,550	1,491	1,287	1,196	1,068	1,133	1,129	1,276
-Public enterprises	1,600	1,780	2,382	2,603	2,848	3,800	4,628	4,474	5,265
-Private sector with public guarantee	30	46	48	76	72	69	62	1,815	2,130
Total public sector	4,275	4,329	5,056	5,242	5,186	5,514	6,666	10,401	13,125
Private sector:									
-Private banks	168	309	660	1,453	3,497	6,629	6,703	4,195	3,469
-Private enterprises	790	975	1,295	1,968	2,524	3,448	3,790	3,441	3,065
Total private sector	958	1,284	1,955	3,421	6,021	10,077	10,493	7,636	6,534
Total external debt	5,233	5,613	7,011	8,663	11,207	15,591	17,159	18,037	19,659
External debt as a percentage of GDP	53.1%	42.0%	45.5%	41.8%	40.6%	47.8%	70.5%	91.3%	102.4%
External debt as a percentage of exports	216.9%	215.6%	238.4%	187.5%	187.8%	311.3%	369.6%	389.7%	455.6%

(1) Includes debt with IMF.

Table 6
Chile: External Debt, 1985–1993
(millions US$)

	1985	1986	1987	1988	1989	1990	1991	1992	1993
Public sector:									
-Central bank (1)	5,442	5,757	6,375	5,243	3,824	3,346	3,062	2,719	2,410
-Treasury	1,990	2,614	2,993	3,512	3,610	3,979	4,279	4,542	4,233
-Public enterprises	5,384	5,312	5,188	4,447	3,965	3,551	2,375	2,141	1,977
-Private sector with public guarantee	2,348	3,408	3,276	2,829	2,120	2,067	1,793	943	912
Total public sector	15,164	17,091	17,832	16,031	13,519	12,943	11,509	10,345	9,532
Private sector:									
-Private banks	2,786	1,463	737	456	623	508	512	2,823	2,928
-Private enterprises	2,579	2,275	2,091	2,473	3,378	5,125	5,298	5,796	7,217
Total private sector	5,365	3,738	2,828	2,929	4,001	5,633	5,810	8,619	10,145
Total external debt	20,529	20,829	20,660	18,960	17,520	18,576	17,319	18,964	19,677
External debt as a percentage of GDP	124.7%	117.6%	99.9%	78.5%	62.4%	61.6%	51.0%	46.0%	44.3%
External debt as a percentage of exports	456.6%	398.0%	327.5%	229.4%	182.2%	180.2%	154.8%	151.4%	164.7%

(1) Includes debt with IMF.

The Chilean external debt almost doubled between 1979 and 1982 (from $8.663 billion to $17.159 billion in 1982. See Table 6.). Of this increment in external debt, private banks participated with 62 percent of the total, private enterprises with 21 percent, public enterprises with 24 percent, and the rest of the public sector actually reduced its external indebtedness (see Table 6). The Chilean central government did not contribute to the increase in the foreign debt at all. In addition, the government had fiscal surpluses during the 1979-1981 period, so there wasn't any fiscal contribution to the current account deficits. Therefore, in the case of Chile, almost all growth in external indebtedness was a private sector phenomenon.

EXTERNAL DEBT CRISIS

The high current account deficits of 1981 and 1982, combined with high real interest rates, led to an explosive external debt path (see Table 6). External debt, which was less than one-half of GDP between 1977 and 1980, started to rise in 1981 in an exponential fashion, surpassing the value of GDP in 1984. At these high debt-GDP ratios, foreign banks perceived a high country risk and did not want to increase their exposure.

As a consequence, the capital inflow declined dramatically: from $4.698 billion in 1981 to $1.215 billion in 1982 and to $508 million in 1983 (see Table 7). In these last two years, almost 40 percent of the reserves were lost. The current account deficit had to be cut to one-fourth, and there was a significant reduction in overall spending.

Since the middle of 1979, Chile had a fixed exchange rate regime with a passive monetary policy. Therefore, the high balance of payments surpluses of 1979 and 1980 implied an expansionary monetary policy in that period. When the capital inflow ceased, and the balance of payments turned into deficit, monetary policy became contractionary. In order to increase the real exchange rate and restore external equilibrium, with a fixed exchange rate regime, a devaluation was needed. Initially, the government tried to maintain the fixed exchange regime and changed labor laws in order to induce a general reduction in nominal wages and prices of non-traded goods. However, price and wage reductions were rather small, and most of the adjustment took place in quantities. Gross domestic product (GDP) fell by -13.6 percent in 1982, and there was massive open unemployment (see Table 8).

In June 1982, the fixed exchange rate regime was abandoned, and a devaluation of 85 percent was implemented over the rest of the year in order to increase the real exchange rate. The rising real exchange rate reversed the previous resource allocation process. The non-tradable sector of the economy, which was "booming" up to 1981, entered a deep crisis. The tradable sector led the recovery process (see Table 9). Many firms operating in the non-traded sector had dollar-denominated debts. The combination of falling activity and

Table 7
Chile: Balance of Payments, 1976–1984
(millions US$)

	1976	1977	1978	1979	1980	1981	1982	1983	1984
Current account:	148	(551)	(1,088)	(1,189)	(1,971)	(4,733)	(2,304)	(1,117)	(2,111)
Capital account:									
-Direct investment	(1)	16	177	233	213	383	401	135	78
-Portfolio investment	(6)	(7)	0	50	(43)	(21)	(17)	(3)	(11)
-Net loans	206	563	1,769	1,964	2,994	4,336	831	376	1,873
Total capital account	199	572	1,946	2,247	3,164	4,698	1,215	508	1,940
Errors and omissions	67	92	(146)	(11)	51	102	(76)	68	188
Balance of payments	414	113	712	1,047	1,244	67	(1,165)	(541)	17

Source: Central Bank.

Table 7, cont.
Chile: Balance of Payments, 1985–1993
(millions US$)

	1985	1986	1987	1988	1989	1990	1991	1992	1993
Current account:	(1,413)	(1,192)	(808)	(167)	(767)	(598)	143	(580)	(2,074)
Capital account:									
-Direct investment	114	116	230	141	184	249	576	739	1,311
-Portfolio investment	28	197	693	870	1,398	766	77	(14)	644
-Net loans	1,242	429	21	(2)	(304)	2,054	160	2,168	713
Total capital account	1,384	742	944	1,009	1,278	3,069	813	2,893	2,668
Errors and omissions	(70)	223	(91)	(110)	(74)	(103)	282	185	(16)
Balance of payments	(99)	(227)	45	732	437	2,368	1,238	2,498	578

Source: Central Bank.

a rising real exchange rate, which indicated a rising real debt, proved to be lethal for many of them. Many firms entered into financial distress, which in turn implied significant numbers of bad loans for the banking system. The biggest banks of Chile became technically bankrupt, and the two largest economic groups (Grupo Cruzat-Larraen and Grupo Vial) entered into financial distress.

Table 8
Chile: Macroeconomic Indicators 1981-1985
(in percentage)

	1981	1982	1983	1984	1985
GDP growth	6.2	-13.6	-2.8	5.9	2.0
Inflation(CPI)	9.5	20.7	23.1	23.0	26.4
Unemployment	11.3	19.6	14.6	13.9	11.9
Fiscal deficit as % of GDP(-)	2.6	-1.0	-2.7	-3.0	-2.3
Ext.debt/GDP	47.8	70.5	91.3	102.4	124.7

Source: Central Bank of Chile.

Table 9
Chile: Absorption and "Crisis" in Non-tradable Sector
(in percentage)

% change in	1982	1983	1984	1985
Absorption	-23.3	-7.2	8.4	-3.4
Real exch. rate	11.5	20.0	4.5	22.8
Real wages	1.6	-13.4	2.5	-11.5
Tradable GDP	-10.9	6.0	8.1	3.9
Non-tradable GDP	-15.1	-4.8	4.5	0.7

Source: Central Bank of Chile.

The danger of massive bankruptcies in the banking system at the beginning of 1983 motivated a governmental intervention in order to support the biggest banks. Grupo Cruzat-Larraen and Grupo Vial were dismantled. Since a significant part of the Chilean external debt was owed by these banks, the state bank's intervention implied a guarantee to the foreign lenders.

In 1983 the economy experienced an additional fall of -2.8 percent in GDP, and real wages fell by -13.4 percent. The economy reached its trough at the middle of 1983 and then started its recovery. The biggest problem was the balance of payments deficit that made it impossible to service the external debt without severe economic disruption.

Chile started its negotiation process with the International Monetary Fund (IMF) in 1982 and with the international banks in 1983. It was extremely difficult to negotiate with five hundred international bank lenders, so an international negotiation committee from these banks was formed. The base of Chilean negotiation was oriented toward external debt restructuring and new money loans in order to finance the balance of payments. New loans for US$780 million from these banks were approved in 1983. Each following year, a new negotiation process was started in order to restructure the external debt again, reduce interest rates, and obtain new loans in order to cover the balance of payments gap.

This negotiation process continued until the country was able to balance its external accounts without any further loans from the foreign banks.

MACROECONOMIC RESPONSE:
EXPORT PROMOTION AND FISCAL ADJUSTMENT

As mentioned before, Chilean economic policy after 1982 was oriented mainly toward solving external overindebtedness. In order to service this high external debt, a reduction of the current account deficit was essential. This was achieved in part by reductions in absorption (see Table 9). But most of Chilean success in dealing with the external debt problem was due to the adoption of an export-led growth strategy.

The key to inducing a general resource allocation toward export-oriented commodities implied setting the relative prices right. For this to occur, a combination of low tariff rates and high real exchange rate was pursued.

In the 1983-1984 crisis, import tariffs went transitorily up from a uniform 10 percent to a uniform 35 percent. However, from 1985 on, all import tariffs were gradually reduced until a uniform 11 percent was reached in 1990. The real exchange rate was maintained at historically high levels.

In order to sustain a high and rising real exchange rate, a contractionary fiscal policy was implemented from 1985 on. Central government expenditures, which represented 30.6 percent of GDP in 1985, went down to 24.4 percent of GDP in 1989 (see Table 10) and further down to 21.3 percent of GDP by 1992. The real exchange rate throughout the period was at a record high by historical standards, and this was combined with low and declining tariff rates.

Table 10
Chile: Fiscal Contraction, Real Exchange Rate,
and Export Performance

	1985	1986	1987	1988	1989
Fiscal expend. as % of GDP	30.6	27.9	26.1	26.4	24.4
Real exch. rate:					
-% change	22.8	10.0	4.3	6.6	-2.3
-Level (1)	149.5	164.5	171.5	182.9	178.6
Export growth:					
-Quantum	13.4	7.7	5.4	7.4	11.5
-Value	4.5	10.4	20.8	38.0	16.2

(1) Base level 1980 = 100.
Sources: IMF Government Finance Statistics and Central Bank of Chile.

As a consequence, relative prices favored the export sector. Most projects implemented during the second half of the 1980s were clearly export oriented. New copper mine ventures were developed; new cellulose plants were constructed, and new fruit plantations covered a significant part of the territory. Chile became the biggest fishmeal exporter in the world and an important salmon exporter. Chilean apples, grapes, and wines became known worldwide.

Figure 1
Exports of Goods and Services
% of GDP

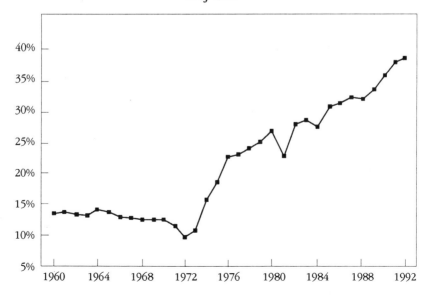

Exports experienced a high growth rate throughout the period.

The export volume had an average growth rate of 9.1 percent per year in the period from 1985 to 1989. Terms of trade also developed favorably, so that the value of exports had a growth rate of 18.0 percent during this period. As a result, the trade balance surplus was growing throughout 1985-1989. In 1985, the trade balance registered a surplus of $884 million and in 1989 of $1.536 billion (see Table 2). This favorable balance of trade path created a growing surplus in the balance of payments from 1987 on (see Table 7).

Table 11
Chile: Macroeconomic Indicators 1986-1989
(in percentage)

	1986	1987	1988	1989
GDP growth	7.4	5.7	7.4	10.0
Inflation (CPI)	17.4	21.5	12.7	21.4
Unemployment	10.8	9.3	8.3	6.3
Fiscal deficit as % of GDP (-)	-0.9	0.4	-0.2	5.0
Ext.debt/GDP	117.6	99.9	78.5	62.4

Source: Central Bank of Chile.

The high rates of growth of the export sector induced an accelerated growth rate in overall GDP. The average rate of growth reached 7.6 percent in the period 1986-1989. The unemployment rate fell throughout the period, and the fiscal deficit turned into a large fiscal surplus in 1989, which reached 5 percent of GDP.

EXTERNAL DEBT STRATEGY:
DEBT-EQUITY SWAPS AND THE USE OF THE SECONDARY MARKET
Creation and Use of a Debt Secondary Market

Since the middle of 1984, some international banks began to sell their Chilean loans with a high discount factor. Some Chilean private investors were willing to buy their debt back at these significant discounts. So, the basis of a secondary market for foreign debt was created. This mechanism became, in some sense, a sort of private market solution to the external debt problem.

However, there were two important institutional barriers that prevented the Chilean private sector from buying back its external debt directly. One barrier was the Chilean foreign exchange system that required the private sector to obtain a prior Central Bank authorization in order to get access to foreign money at the official exchange rate. The Central Bank was not in a condition to authorize such operations, since the country was experiencing severe balance of payments deficits. Authorizing a capital outflow would just increase these problems. Another alternative for that purpose was to authorize the use of the black market for foreign exchange. This alternative had an important disadvantage: It could create excessive pressure in the dollar black market, inducing a rise in the black market-official exchange rate differential. A big exchange rate differential would mean a high incentive to underinvoice exports and overinvoice imports, which would in turn cause the balance of payments to deteriorate.

The second barrier consisted of certain specific clauses contained in the restructuring agreements made with the bank lenders, which imposed the "sharing" principle: All lenders had to be paid in proportion, and nobody could receive anticipated payment.

The economic authorities decided that the use of a secondary market for external debt was an attractive alternative for solving the debt problem. The private sector could, in principle, buy this debt back and use these resources in new investments or in debt reduction. For this to occur, both barriers had to be removed. The first barrier was easy: The Central Bank designated several programs for external debt conversion. The second barrier was negotiated with the foreign banks in order to change the appropriate clauses.

The macroeconomic consequences of using domestic money to buy the debt back or inviting foreign investors for this same purpose were very different. Therefore, two different legal conversion mechanisms were designated: one for domestic investors (Chapter XVIII) and one for foreigners (Chapter XIX).

In addition, a special mechanism for using debt-equity swaps in the foreign investment law (DL 600) was designed. Other special programs for reducing private sector indebtedness or using Central Bank reserves to buy their debt back were used from time to time.

These mechanisms were quite successful in reducing a substantial part of the Chilean external debt. Total debt conversion in the period 1985 to 1993 reached $11.314 billion (about 25.4 percent of 1993 GDP). In September 1993, Chile's total external debt was $19.753 billion (about 44.4 percent of 1993 GDP). Had these debt conversion programs not taken place, Chile's total external debt would have been 57 percent higher in 1993.

Of the different conversion mechanisms used, the biggest success stories were Chapter XVIII, which concentrated 29.0 percent of total debt conversions, and Chapter XIX with 31.8 percent. Another important mechanism was direct buy-backs of debt, which reached $1.458 billion (12.8 percent of total) and is classified in other programs (see Table 12). Total debt conversions were relatively modest in the beginning (only $330 million in 1985) but increased with exponential speed in the following years (see Table 13).

Table 12
Chile: External Debt Conversion Programs
(millions US$)

	Debt-Equity Swap (DL 600)	Chapter XVIII	Chapter XIX	External Debt-Int. Debt Swap	Other Programs	Total
1985	53	115	32	41	89	330
1986	56	411	214	27	276	984
1987	125	696	707	–	451	1,979
1988	52	909	886	67	856	2,770
1989	2	410	1,321	20	929	2,682
1990	16	592	418	–	71	1,097
1991	–	147	22	–	659	828
1992	–	–	–	–	385	385
1993	4	–	–	–	255	259
Total	308	3,280	3,600	155	3,971	11,314

Notes: Figures correspond to the face value of external debt converted in each year.
1993 figure corresponds to the period January - September of that year.
Source: Central Bank.

Table 13
Chile: External Debt Converted by Debtor
(millions US$)

	Debt-Equity Swap (DL 600)	Chapter XVIII	Chapter XIX	External Debt-Int. Debt Swap	Other Programs	Total
Public sector:						
-Central bank	–	729	1,124	27	698	2,578
-Treasury	–	–	–	–	69	69
-Public enterprises	–	469	403	43	1,135	2,050
-Private sector with public guarantee	2	1,908	2,050	82	494	4,536
Total public sector	2	3,106	3,577	152	2,396	9,233
Private sector:						
-Private banks	166	85	22	–	117	390
-Private enterprises	140	89	1	3	1,458	1,691
Total private sector	306	174	23	3	1,575	2,081
Total	308	3,280	3,600	155	3,971	11,314

Source: Central Bank.

The largest debt reduction took place using private sector debt instruments with public guarantees (about 40.0 percent of total conversions). Other important sources of external debt instruments came from the Central Bank (about 22.8 percent of total conversions) and from public enterprises (about 18.1 percent of total conversions). Private sector debt instruments without public guarantees played a minor role in debt conversions. Only 14.9 percent of total conversions used debt instruments issued by private enterprises, and 3.4 percent used debt instruments issued by private banks (see Table 12).

When the external debt-GDP ratio began to decline, the price of Chilean debt in the secondary market began to rise (see Table 14), reducing the incentives for using debt conversion mechanisms. Therefore, debt conversions declined markedly after 1990. The last debt conversions using Chapter XVIII or XIX took place in 1991. The biggest conversion operations took place in 1988 and 1989, with an average price of external debt instruments of about 60 percent (see Table 14).[1]

Table 14
Chile: Price of External Debt in the Secondary Market
(in percentage)

Year	External Debt in Secondary Market	External Debt-GDP ratio
1986	66.7	117.6
1987	69.7	99.9
1988	59.0	78.5
1989	60.0	62.4
1990	67.0	61.6
1991	84.0	51.0
1992	89.0	46.0
1993	93.0	44.5

Sources: CEPAL and financial newspapers.

Mechanism for Domestic Investors: Chapter XVIII

Chapter XVIII was specially designed for domestic investors so that they could officially buy Chilean external debt instruments. These debt instruments could be presented to the original debtors in order to convert this debt back into pesos or another domestic-denominated debt. The original debtors could also use this mechanism to buy back their own debt.

These investors did not have access to the official foreign exchange market. Instead, they had to use the black market for foreign exchange in order to obtain the dollars to buy the foreign debt instruments. The black market received a legal status and turned into a free market for foreign exchange.

In order to avoid a high free market-official exchange rate differential, a periodic quota for debt conversions was established. Quotas were fixed twice a month, and the right to join was auctioned by the Central Bank.[2] By fixing the level of each quota, the Central Bank had indirect control over the free market-official exchange rate spread. This spread was never allowed to widen beyond 15 percent (see Table 15).

Most of the dollars sold in the Chilean free market were funded from foreign deposits of the Chilean private sector. Chapter XVIII had the effect of bringing these resources back to the country.

Table 15
Chile: Free Market-Official Exchange Rate Spread

Year	Free Market Exchange Rate $/US$	Official Exchange Rate $/US$	Exchange Rate Spread %
1985	180.91	157.41	14.93
1986	205.02	192.93	6.27
1987	230.12	219.41	4.88
1988	281.83	245.01	15.03
1989	298.11	266.37	11.92
1990	312.29	304.95	2.41
1991	354.90	349.00	1.69

Source: Central Bank of Chile.

A typical Chapter XVIII operation was performed through the private banking system or some specialized agents. It involved several fees for the different economic agents that intervened in the different steps of the process. First, there was a small fee for the private bank (or agent) that managed the process. Then, there was another small fee for the foreign broker that acquired the foreign debt instruments. Third, there was an important fee paid to the Central Bank for getting a place in the quota auction. Finally, the original debtors also got a part of the benefit, since they could buy (redenominate) their debt back at less than its face value. Average fees and discounts for Chapter XVIII in different years are shown in Table 16.

Table 16
Chile: Fees and Discounts for Chapter XVIII
(in percent of face value)

Year	Debt Discount (1)	Central Bank Fee (2)	Debtor Discount (3)	Exchange Spread (4)	Others (5)
1985	34.1	2.7	8.0	13.8	9.6
1986	32.7	10.9	9.0	8.0	4.8
1987	38.4	20.5	11.5	4.7	1.7
1988	40.1	15.1	12.0	12.9	0.1
1989	39.8	6.7	16.1	10.7	6.3
1990	32.6	6.0	19.2	2.4	5.0

(1) Debt discount was implicit in debt valuation in the secondary market.
(2) Fees received by the Central Bank in the quota auction.
(3) Part of the discount was received by the original debtor as a debt redenomination.
(4) Corresponds to the free market-official market exchange rate difference expressed as a percentage of debt face value.
(5) This figure includes brokers' fees and profits from Chapter XVIII operations.
Source: Central Bank of Chile.

Taking 1989 as an example (see Table 16), an average Chapter XVIII operation in that year bought debt instruments at a 39.8 percent discount. This means that debt instruments for $1,000 face value were bought for $602 in the secondary market. Therefore, it obtained a $398 gross benefit for each $1,000 of face value. However, in order to get access to the Chapter XVIII quota from the Central Bank, it had to pay a fee of 6.7 percent of the face value of debt, which means $67 for each $1,000 of face value. The benefit, after payment of the Central Bank fee, was reduced to $331 for each $1,000 of face value. Finally, the investor had to receive the money from the original debtors, who also received a share of the benefits. The average debtor discount was 16.1 percent in that year, which means that the debtors were willing to buy back their own debt (probably funded with a new debt given by the agent bank) at $839 for each $1,000 of face value. Only $170 for each $1,000 of face value was left after deducting the debtor discount. From this figure, another $20 had to be deducted for bank and brokerage fees, leaving only $150 of benefit for each $1,000 of face value. If the investors had the dollars, they could earn a 24.9 percent benefit from this operation ($150/$602). However, if they started with Chilean pesos, they had to acquire dollars in the free market, and the debt was paid at the official exchange rate. They had to deduct the exchange rate spread, which was 10.7 percent in 1989 (see Table 16). Therefore, the final benefit from the operation was $43 ($150 minus $107), or 7.1 percent of the amount invested.

Of the $3.133 billion in debt converted by Chapter XVIII in the period 1985 to 1990, the total debt discount in the secondary market amounted to

$1.162 billion (37.1 percent of the face value of debt). This total benefit of $1.162 billion was distributed in the following way: 33.6 percent accrued to the Central Bank in the form of quota fees ($391 million); another 35.7 percent accrued to the original debt holders as a reduction in their debt ($415 million); 22.1 percent went to pay the free market-official exchange rate difference ($257 million); 5.4 percent served to pay banking and brokerage fees ($63 million), and finally only 3.2 percent was the pure profit component obtained by the private investors ($36 million or 5.1 percent of the amount invested).

Some special programs were defined in the context of Chapter XVIII. One such program was Annex 4 of Chapter XVIII, which allowed Chilean investors to capitalize enterprises and banks in financial distress without paying the quota fee to the Central Bank. This operation was applicable only to the final debtor and required explicit approval of the Central Bank. Total operations implemented under Annex 4 amounted to $208 million.

Another special program was Annex 5 of Chapter XVIII. This program was created in March 1988 in order to finance a general rescheduling of housing mortgages. Only external debt instruments issued by the Central Bank could be used for this purpose. Total debt conversions under Annex 5 amounted to $378 million.

Mechanism for Foreign Investors: Chapter XIX

Chapter XIX was created for foreign investors so that they could buy Chilean debt instruments in the secondary market, exchange these debt instruments for Chilean pesos or instruments denominated in pesos, and invest them in Chile. Only debt instruments of public entities or those having a public guarantee were eligible for this kind of operation.

Foreign investors using Chapter XIX were given access to the official exchange rate for sending their profits and capital back in the future. Chapter XIX required foreign investors to keep profits in Chile for a minimum period of four years. From the fifth year on, investors were allowed to remit all profits of that year plus 25 percent of the accumulated profits from the first four years. In the tenth year, they were allowed to remit even the capital back.

Since the spirit of Chapter XIX was to induce new foreign investment in the country, each operation was explicitly examined and approved by the Central Bank on a case-by-case basis. This examination tried to determine whether the foreign investors were really "foreign" or whether they were Chilean investors trying to benefit from the more favorable treatment of Chapter XIX. The Central Bank also tried to determine whether the investment was really new or whether it was an investment that would have taken place even without this incentive. A third aspect closely examined was the nature of the project. Projects that were export oriented or that helped to capitalize a firm in financial distress were given preference. The analysis also tried to detect investors who might implement "hit and run" strategies in order to avoid them.

Chapter XIX operations generated $3.600 billion, of which 31.8 percent corresponds to total debt conversions. Most of the foreign investors came from the United States, with around 38.8 percent of total Chapter XIX operations up to 1990 (see Table 17). Other important sources of funds came from Great Britain (12.6 percent) and New Zealand (11.2 percent). Chapter XIX foreign investors came from 35 different countries around the world (see Table 17).

Table 17
Chile: Origin of Chapter XIX Operations
(in percent of total)

Country	Percent
United States	38.78
Great Britain	12.57
New Zealand	11.22
Spain	6.41
France	3.74
Sweden	3.43
Saudi Arabia	2.57
Canada	2.25
Netherlands	1.86
Switzerland	1.76
Italy	1.73
Kuwait	1.49
Japan	1.44
Panama	1.31
Cayman Islands	1.31
South Africa	1.10
Others	7.03
Total	100.00

Source: Central Bank of Chile.

Most of the Chapter XIX foreign investment resources went to the industrial sector (39 percent of total), especially the pulp, paper, and food industries. Another important destination was agriculture (around 21 percent), especially fruit production and forestry. The mining sector received more than 11 percent of total investments in order to open new mines. The banking sector received around 6 percent of total investments, which served to capitalize some bankrupt banks. Chapter XIX was also significant for the communications sector, which received a little less than 6 percent of total investments. This last operation allowed for the privatization of the local telephone company and served as the basis for an ambitious expansion plan in the telecommunications area (see Table 18).

A special program known as Annex 2 of Chapter XIX gave special facilities to foreign investors so that they could buy foreign debt instruments and use this money in the capitalization of existing enterprises. Each operation required a prior approval from the Central Bank. A total of $130 million in debt was converted by this program.

Table 18
Chile: Destination of Chapter XIX Operations
(in percent of total)

Sector	Percent
Agriculture	20.98
Fishery	4.36
Mining	11.24
Industry	39.00
Electricity	1.52
Commerce	2.99
Hotels	2.82
Transport	0.53
Communications	5.77
Banking	6.11
Insurance	3.72
Services	0.96
Total	100.00

Source: Central Bank of Chile.

Other Conversion Programs

One of the less successful stories was the debt-equity swap program defined in the context of the foreign investment law (DL 600). Only $308 million of foreign debt was converted with this program, which represented less than 3 percent of total debt conversions, most of them related to private banks and enterprises (see Table 13).

Another unsuccessful program was the external debt-internal debt swap, which represented about $155 million of foreign debt conversions, little more than 1.3 percent of the total.

An interesting conversion mechanism was used by the Central Bank. Since the Central Bank had a comfortable reserve position, it used part of these reserves to buy back its own debt directly. An international auction was held for that purpose, and the Central Bank bought around $440 million of its own debt at an average discount of 42.2 percent.

In 1989, the Chilean fruit producers suffered serious damage due to a worldwide fruit embargo that started in the United States. There was an allegation by the U.S. Food and Drug Administration (FDA) of fruit poisoning that later proved to be false. In order to alleviate part of the damage to Chilean fruit producers, a special debt conversion program was defined for them. This program (Agreement 1924-01 of the Central Bank) allowed Chilean fruit exporters to convert foreign debt instruments up to the amount of exports made in the period February-April 1989. A total of $357 million was converted at an average discount of 40 percent.

Other special programs were defined by Clauses 5.11 and 5.12 of the external debt renegotiation program. These clauses allowed firms undergoing privatization to repay external debt in pesos. Since these firms were state owned, their debt was classified as public. A total debt conversion of $894 million was achieved through this program.

Although it was not officially allowed, many private enterprises acquired their own debt instruments directly, without paying any quota rights to the Central Bank and without any official approval. In these cases, they were able to get most of the benefits from the secondary market discount. These unofficial operations added up to $1.458 billion of external debt instruments (at face value) and are officially classified under "other programs" (see Table 12).

THE END OF THE DEBT CRISIS

In 1991, the debt crisis in Chile was almost over. The external debt-GDP ratio was 51 percent and declined to about 44.5 percent by 1993 (see Table 6). The capital account of the balance of payments returned to very high inflow levels, which induced a growing current account deficit. The net capital inflow was $813 million in 1991, $2.893 billion in 1992, and $2.840 billion in 1993. The current account reached a surplus equivalent to 0.4 percent of GDP in 1991 and to a deficit of 1.4 percent of GDP in 1992 (see Table 2).

In 1992, the Chilean economy exported $12.526 billion in goods and services, which was almost 2.7 times the level of 1982 ($4.642 billion). Its gross domestic product in dollar terms was 1.7 times bigger (from $24.340 billion in 1982 to $41.203 billion in 1992), yet its total external debt was only 10 percent higher in dollar terms (from $17.159 billion in 1982 to $18.964 billion in 1992).

In addition, the balance of payments showed positive surpluses each year from 1987 to 1993. This implied a continuous accumulation of Central Bank gross reserves that reached a level of $10.426 billion in 1993. This level of reserves is enough to finance almost one year of imports and constitutes an historic record.

The level of net indebtedness of the country, defined as the total debt less Central Bank reserves, actually declined by more than one-third between 1982 and 1992 (from $14.575 billion in 1982 to $9.233 billion in 1992). Chile was increasingly perceived as a stable and low-risk country by the international financial community, and this reflected in a growing capital inflow for both investment and debt purposes.

Finally, the growth performance of the Chilean economy was notable. After a slowdown in 1990, induced by a contractionary monetary policy which reduced the growth rate to 3.0 percent, the economy accelerated again to 6.1 percent in 1991 and 10.3 percent in 1992. For 1993, the growth rate remained high at 5.9 percent. In summary, the external debt crisis was solved by a combination of macroeconomic policies oriented toward fiscal discipline, development policies oriented toward export-led growth, and debt conversion policies oriented toward converting debt into equity. The end result was not only the solution to the external debt problem but a healthier and more competitive economy.

Notes

1. The significant drop in the price of Chilean debt from 1987 (69.7 percent) to 1988 (59.0 percent) can be explained by a "Latin American" effect. In the same year, the price of Argentinean debt dropped from 50.3 percent in 1987 to 26.0 percent in 1988, due to the failure of the "Austral Plan," and the price of Brazilian debt dropped from 60.0 percent to 46.0 percent, due to the failure of the "Cruzado Plan."

2. Interested investors offered the Central Bank a fee in order to participate in the given quota. This offer had to be made in a closed envelope and was kept secret. The Central Bank arranged the offers in order from the highest to the lowest, until the quota was accomplished.

3. An IMD of Switzerland study classifies Chile as a low-risk country, and it ranked in fifth place in international competitiveness in 1993, only after the "Asian Dragons" (*World Competitiveness Report 1993*, IMD, Switzerland).

III

BRAZIL'S ROLLERCOASTER RESPONSE TO THE DEBT CRISIS

Carlos von Doellinger

From 1964 to the mid-1970s, Brazil was able to sustain the highest rates of GDP growth among developing countries. The growth rates accelerated from an average 3.9 percent, during the 1964-1967 period, to 10.5 percent during the so-called "economic wonder" of the 1968-1974 period. This performance has been attributed to the results of stabilization policies implemented during the 1964-1967 period, as well as to a wide range of economic reforms.

Starting in April 1964, the conventional monetary and fiscal policies decreased annual inflation rates from 144 percent (1964) to 25 percent (1967).

The economic reforms were designed to improve government finances, to recover the international demand for Brazilian exports, and to achieve higher savings and investment rates. The reforms and the economic performance itself produced not only higher investment rates (and GDP growth) but also remarkable inflows of foreign resources. Table 1 displays savings and investment rates as percentages of GDP for different subperiods.

Table 1
Brazil: Savings and Investment Rates as Percentages of GDP

Time Periods	1960-1964	1965-1967	1968-1974	1975-1981
Total investment/ savings	21.7	22.5	22.6	23.3
External savings	1.6	-0.2	2.4	4.9
National savings	*20.1*	*22.7*	*20.2*	*18.4*
Public sector	0.9	3.2	5.5	1.5
Private sector	19.2	19.5	14.7	16.9

Source: Inter-American Development Bank, Country Studies Division.

The most striking feature is the jump in the nation's use of foreign savings. After averaging -0.2 percent of GDP in the 1965-1967 period, the external savings reached 2.4 percent in the 1968-1974 period and 4.9 percent in the 1975-1981 period.

Since most of the foreign resources were in the form of loans, the Brazilian foreign debt jumped from $3.1 billion in December 1964 to $19 billion in 1974 and $43 billion in 1978, immediately before the second oil shock.

Notwithstanding the fact that government savings increased in relation to GDP, it seems clear that external resources not only added to the domestic savings capacity but also emerged as a substitute for domestic private savings. This is especially true for the 1964-1974 time span, during which consumption outlays rose at rates equal to or even higher than GDP growth.

In short, high growth rates were sustained by investments, financed by increasing proportions of foreign savings. External debt accumulated faster than GDP growth. That was the strategy of "growth-with-debt" in Brazil, from the mid-1960s to the second oil crisis (Table 2).

Table 2
Foreign Debt and GDP in Brazil in Selected Years
(in billions US$)

	1964	1968	1974	1978
GDP (1)	28.249	34.940	84.019	20.200
Foreign debt (2)	3.101	3.780	19.400	43.600
(2)/(1)	10.97%	10.81%	23.09%	26.53%

(2)/(1) = Foreign debt as % of GDP.
Source: Central Bank of Brazil, Annual Reports.

ECONOMIC POLICY TOWARD "ROLL-OVER"

The "growth-with-debt" strategy had negative consequences even before the second oil shock and the debt crisis of the early 1980s. The substantial growth of the external debt, nearly tripling in a period of just five years between the first and second oil shocks (1974-1978), was accompanied by sharply increased servicing requirements (interest payments and amortizations). Debt servicing rose from $3.3 billion in 1974 (38 percent of exports) to $8.6 billion in 1978 (62.3 percent of exports). The country serviced that debt by acquiring new loans, contracted at variable interest rates.

Variable rates were not a problem until 1979. Real rates had been low and even negative in some years. Such conditions changed dramatically during the 1979-1981 period, when Brazil's external debt continued to expand at an accelerated pace in the context of a deteriorating economic situation. In the face of a slow-down in export growth, rising oil prices, and huge increases in international interest rates, it became increasingly difficult to meet debt service obligations through the contracting of new loans.

Despite these increasing difficulties, the Brazilian government was able to sustain the process until 1981, when foreign debt reached $65.1 billion. Foreign branches of Brazilian commercial banks were mobilized, as were state-owned enterprises. The nation also began to make growing use of short-term financing through the interbank markets. Rising proportions of debt became concentrated in the public sector.

The first government response to that situation was the adoption of restrictive monetary policies at the end of 1980. The policies were aimed at bringing about an internal adjustment to the new environment.

Making use of conventional monetary instruments, the government succeeded in curbing domestic demand. In 1981, GDP experienced its first real decline since World War II (-4.4 percent). The trade balance (merchandise and non-factor services) improved from a negative $5.9 billion in 1980 to a negative $1.6 billion in 1981 (Table 3). Unfortunately, the current account did not improve accordingly. The stabilization policies adopted by the United States caused international interest rates to soar again. As a consequence, interest payments jumped from $7.4 billion in 1980 to $10.4 billion in 1981.

Tight monetary policies were continued in 1982, but increasing debt service obligations created additional difficulties for the balance of payments and, consequently, for access to international markets.

Brazil's access to markets became further restricted in the third quarter of 1982, in the wake of the debt crisis in Mexico. The country continued to honor the debt, but in the absence of new loans, its international reserve position decreased to almost zero by December 1982.

The fundamental government responses remained — the reinforcement of conventional policies required to achieve an internal adjustment to the new, unfavorable circumstances in international markets. For this purpose, the country started negotiations with the International Monetary Fund (IMF) for an Extended Fund Facility Arrangement. Debt negotiations with the Paris Club and the private banks also took place at the same time, together with the contracting of short-term bridge loans to restore the reserve position. The main purpose of these concerted actions was the debt "roll-over."

These efforts mobilized enough financing for the 1982 current deficit by relying on expensive short-term loans. Thus, the foreign debt increased to $91.9 billion. The ratio of debt service to exports jumped again to 98.5 percent, the highest level in history (Table 4).

This situation was largely alleviated during the period 1983-1984, due to some fundamental adjustments in the economy imposed by the IMF program. As shown in Tables 3 and 4, the foreign sector improved substantially in 1983 and 1984.

Table 3
Brazil's Balance of Payments
(in billions US$)

	1978	1979	1980	1981	1982	1983	1984
Trade balance	-2.871	-5.025	-5.928	-1.632	-2.803	-4.092	-11.364
Non-factor serv.	-1.715	-2.318	-3.117	-2.877	-3.592	-2.394	-1.750
Merch. exp. (FOB)	12.450	15.235	20.140	23.342	20.189	21.923	27.050
Merch. imp. (FOB)	13.606	17.942	22.951	22.100	19.400	15.437	13.936
Balance of factor payments	-4.232	-5.459	-7.032	-10.325	-13.521	-10.997	-11.482

Source: Central Bank of Brazil, Annual Reports.

Table 4
Foreign Debt Indicators in Brazil
(in billions US$)

	1978	1979	1980	1981	1982	1983	1984
Total debt	53.6	60.4	70.6	80.4	91.9	97.5	104.7
Debt service	8.6	11.6	14.1	17.9	20.6	12.9	13.9
Interests	3.3	5.3	7.5	10.4	12.6	10.3	11.5
Amortizations	5.3	6.3	6.6	7.5	8.0	2.6	2.1
Relationships							
Debt serv./exp. (%)	62.3	69.3	64.5	69.7	98.5	54.4	46.9
Debt/exports (%)	388.1	361.2	322.2	313.6	417.6	412.1	361.0
Debt/GDP (%)	26.8	27.2	30.0	30.3	32.3	47.2	49.1

Source: Central Bank of Brazil, Annual Reports.

The contraction of domestic demand, mainly the consolidated public deficit reduction, created conditions for the rise of exports and the fall of imports. Amortizations were sharply cut, since the government succeeded in the "rolling over" of the debt. In 1983, they represented less than one-fourth of total disbursements made in 1982. With the exception of debt/GDP, all ratios improved during the 1983-1984 period. Table 5 shows the domestic adjustment indicators, which followed the Letter of Intent approved by the IMF board in November 1983.

Table 5
Brazil: Indicators of Domestic Adjustment

	1981	1982	1983	1984
Public sector borrowing requirements *(PSBR - public deficit, in % of GDP)*	5.9	6.6	3.0	1.6
Gross domestic savings *(in % of GDP)*	20.8	19.4	17.1	21.7
GDP growth rates	-3.1	1.1	-2.8	5.7
International reserves in Central Bank *(in billions US$)*	7.507	3.994	4.563	11.995

Source: Central Bank of Brazil, Annual Reports.

The consolidated public deficit went down to 1.6 percent of GDP, from a peak of 6.6 percent in 1982. Domestic savings recovered to 21.7 percent of GDP, allowing a GDP growth rate of 5.7 percent in 1984. International reserves in the Central Bank rose from less than $4 billion in 1982 to $12 billion in 1984.

These indicators gave support to the following foreword in a Central Bank quarterly report: "Success was obtained for many important goals in the economic adjustment program in 1984, particularly in the external sector, in the operational concept of the public deficit, and in the net domestic assets. However, there was less success in reaching targets for the growth of the monetary aggregates and inflation."[1]

CONFRONTATION STRATEGIES: 1985-1987

The tightening of economic policies during 1983-1984 resulted in disparate consequences. Some surpassed the targets of the stabilization program, but others fell far short of expectations. The government succeeded in restoring the external gap. The cost, however, was rising unemployment and recession in 1983. The recovery of 1984 was not sufficient to bring income levels back to the 1980 level. The 1984 growth was due mostly to the soaring recovery of exports and agricultural harvest, and it was largely insufficient to reduce unemployment. The investment rates continued to fall.

The government's significant progress in adjusting the balance of payments was tarnished by the singular failure to control inflation. Inflation rates, measured by the General Price Index,[2] remained at levels higher than 200 percent per year, despite the apparently successful control of the public deficit. The financial gap in the consolidated government account was considered the main original source of inflation in Brazil but was aggravated by the indexation process of prices, wages, exchange rates, and interest rates.

As a matter of fact, the reduction in the "operational deficit"[3] had not been followed by the same trend in the "nominal deficit," measured by the nominal increases in the consolidated public debt (both domestic and external). In other words, the nominal public sector borrowing requirements continued to soar, from 16.6 percent of GDP in 1982, to 19.9 percent in 1983, and 22.1 percent in 1984, as a consequence of inflation and indexation.

Government failures in curbing inflation and unemployment gave rise to strong political pressures against economic policies "imposed" by the IMF. The elections of November 1984 gave the presidency to the strongest opposition party, the Partido do Movimento Democrático Brasileiro (PMDB).[4] The motto of the PMDB had been a famous public statement by the newly elected president, Tancredo Neves: "The external debt should never be paid with the blood of Brazilian people."

Tancredo Neves died in April 1985, and the vice president, José Sarney, took over the presidency. After an initial period of ambivalence, the economic policies began to change during the second half of 1985. These policies were characterized by a full acceptance of new priorities imposed by the PMDB economists: economic recovery, employment growth, higher government investments, and the "renegotiation" of the external debt in order to provide room for a stronger rebound in domestic demand.

A principal result of the emerging policy orientation was precisely the strong recovery of domestic demand, which was the main source of the 8 percent GDP growth in 1985, the largest increase in six years. Luckily enough, the 1985 recovery was obtained with almost no deterioration in Brazil's external situation, due to decreases in international interest rates and oil prices.

Domestic demand was led by investment, which recovered by 19.9 percent in 1985, and domestic private consumption, which jumped more than 3 percent in real terms. Given those favorable external conditions, the domestic demand increase was offset by a decrease in foreign demand.

Inflation, however, remained at extremely high levels, with prices escalating steadily in the closing months of the year and in the early months of 1986.

To an extent, the intensification of inflation was a predictable consequence of a domestic demand upturn. It was also a consequence of the rise in the public deficit, which reached 4.3 percent of GDP using the operational concept of the IMF and 27.5 percent in "nominal" terms. This upsurge resulted from a higher public sector wage bill (due both to higher wages and employment), rising interest rates on the domestic debt caused by strong government demand for financial funds, and the hike in subsidies resulting from price controls.

This situation deteriorated in early 1986, giving the impression of a steady drift toward hyperinflation.

The ministers, politicians, and economists of the PMDB explained the deteriorating situation as a mere consequence of the indexation process (the so-called "inertial" component of inflation) and the rise in government expenditures caused by interest payments, which soared due to the increased servicing requirements of both domestic and foreign debt. This kind of argument provided the "rationale" for the Cruzado Plan (February 28, 1986), the first in a sequence of five "non-orthodox"[5] experiments to eliminate inflation and restore economic growth.

The principal measures of this first plan, which were also included in at least three of the other four experiments,[6] are listed below:

- A new monetary unit was introduced.

- Monetary correction on most types of financial assets was abolished.

- The indexed treasury bond (ORTN), the key indexed security in the economy, was abolished and replaced by the nonindexed National Treasury Bond (OTN).

- Wages and incomes were converted into cruzados on the basis of their average real value (as opposed to peak values) during the preceding six months.

- A few prices, including public utilities tariffs, were adjusted and then frozen for an indefinite period, together with all prices of goods and services.

The consequences of the Cruzado Plan during 1986 were highly disparate, but by year-end, and during the early months of 1987, it became increasingly unfavorable. By June 1987, it was a complete failure.

During 1986, the plan did result in a slowdown of inflation, but it also triggered a boom in private consumption, which rose 10.9 percent in real terms.

Domestic supply was not sufficient to meet demand, even with the help of a strong decline in exports and a real increase in imports. The situation was aggravated by a 6.2 percent decline in agriculture. Investment, despite rising by 22.2 percent, was also insufficient to reduce capacity constraints. Industry boomed at 14.1 percent as a consequence of domestic demand for consumer goods as well as housing, which experienced an unbelievable 19.8 percent growth.

Inflation resumed after the November elections of 1986, which gave still more power to the PMDB. Together with inflation, the balance of payments was adversely affected. The trade balance, having registered an average surplus of $12.8 billion in 1984-1985, dropped to only $8.3 billion, due largely to a decline in exports of more than 12 percent.

This poor performance was attributable to the diversion of exports to the domestic market (to meet soaring consumption). Imports were also affected.

The government tried to offset the pressure on domestic markets and prices using imported goods. Since the exchange rate remained fixed from March to mid-October, imports were considered a tool to keep prices under control. Not only commodities but also raw materials and capital goods contributed to a 6.7 percent rise in total imports, notwithstanding the decline in petroleum imports from $5.77 billion in 1985 to $2.8 billion in 1986. The final result was a $4.39 billion current account deficit, much higher than the average of $142 million during 1984-1985. As shown in Table 6, all macroeconomic indicators deteriorated during the 1985-1987 period. By the end of 1986, inflationary expectations accelerated because of the reintroduction of indexation of assets and wages. The exchange rate had been regularly adjusted since October. Consequently, when the price freeze was officially lifted in February 1987, prices immediately jumped 30 to 40 percent. As shown in Table 6, inflation soared again to 415.8 percent in 1987.

The external sector was particularly affected by the uncertainties that came about in late 1986 and early 1987. In particular, the drying up of capital flows, the increasing deterioration in the trade balance, and the fall in reserves (Table 7) resulted in difficulties in servicing the debt. In February 1987, the government decided to suspend interest payments due to $68 billion of external debt with the private sector (Debt Moratorium of February 1987).

Table 6
Brazil: Selected Economic Indicators (1985-1987)

	1985	1986	1987
PSBR - operational concept			
(in % of GDP) (surplus + or deficit -)-4.3	-3.5	-3.5	-5.7
Inflation - General Price Index (%)	235.1	65.0	415.8
GDP - annual growth in (%)	8.4	8.0	2.9
Trade balance (FOB)	107.16m	6.312b	8.911b
(in millions/billions US$)			
Disbursed external debt	106.473	112.767	123.962
(in billions US$)			

Source: Central Bank of Brazil, Annual Reports.

The stated reasons given by the government to the international banking community and to public opinion revolved around the untenability of servicing the debt. Also, debt rescheduling was supposed to be worked out. The decision, in any case, was a predictable outcome of the new economic policy. It ushered in a period of confrontation and a new government response to the debt problem. The "moratorium" lasted 18 months. In September 1988, after another failure by the second non-orthodox stabilization experiment (Plano Bresser), the government decided to reintroduce orthodox monetary and fiscal policies and resume interest payments.

Table 7
Brazil: Foreign Reserves and Trade Balance
(millions/billions US$)

1986	Trade Balance (FOB)	Reserves (liquidity concept)
June	1.070b	10.391b
July	1.005b	9.499b
August	945m	9.105b
September	533m	9.025b
October	-83m	8.006b
November	-38m	7.347b
December	-217m	6.760b
1987		
January	-35m	5.380b
February	320m	4.965b

FOB = free on board.
Source: Central Bank of Brazil, Annual Reports.

1988: NEW ATTEMPTS TO RESUME "ORTHODOX" POLICIES AND DEBT SERVICE

On September 21, 1988, the Central Bank revoked the moratorium on external debt interest payments. On September 22, 1988, a multiyear agreement was concluded with commercial banks. The major points of the agreement included the following:

1. Rescheduling of 94 percent of the medium- and long-term debt maturing in the period 1987-1993 (including the amounts maturing in 1986), totaling $60.6 billion, over a period of 20 years and an eight-year grace period;

2. Acceptance by the private bank lenders of a new spread (maximum) of 13 to 26 percent;

3. Interest payments on a half-year basis;

4. "New money" of $5.2 billion, with a 12-year term and a five-year grace period;

5. Longer term for short-term lines (commercial and interbank), totaling $14.1 billion;

6. Switching from the interbank project line to trade lines of $600 million; and

7. Relending of the new resources deposited in the Central Bank (D.F.A.). Relending to the private sector with a minimum term of six years, with a five-year grace period.

It appeared that Brazil had reached the end of an 18-month period of belligerency and increasing difficulties in the external sector. As a matter of fact, the economic environment improved somewhat during the first half of 1988, due to tight monetary policies imposed by Minister Mailson da Nobrega. Nobrega took these actions in December 1987 after the failure of a second attempt at freezing prices.[7] The government response to the debt crisis turned again to "orthodoxy."

To a large extent, the agreement with private banks was an outcome of a rapprochement with the IMF, after three years of estrangement from the institution. By early June, the country had already presented an adjustment program to the IMF staff. The program, which was approved on June 29, 1988, included a 19-month stand-by agreement for a loan of $1.4 billion.

The main target of the program was a cut in the "operational" public deficit to 4 percent of GDP in 1988 (from 6 percent in 1987), down to 2 percent in 1989. The program also stipulated that inflation should not be higher than 600 percent in 1988 and monetary expansion be limited to 375 percent. Real growth of the domestic debt should not exceed 5 percent.

Renegotiations with the IMF also led to a new agreement with the Paris Club during August 1988, which resulted in the rescheduling of medium- and long-term debt with bilateral creditors. At the same time, the negotiations facilitated access to short-term credit lines for trade operations, which had been suspended, together with all kinds of external financing.

The rapprochement with the international financial system benefited the external sector in 1988. The balance of payments improved. By September, the country had already achieved its goal of a $12.6 billion trade surplus scheduled to be reached in December. By year-end, the surplus surpassed an historical high of $19 billion. The target for international reserves was also surpassed, and the foreign debt was reduced by $10 billion through debt-equity conversions.

Despite these positive results, the country failed again on the domestic front. As in 1983-1984, inflation escalated to a level of 934 percent — so far the highest rate in the nation's history. Real GDP declined 0.3 percent, and real wages went down despite the monthly indexation.[8] Unemployment rose, and the social costs seemed to be unbearable again. Among the factors contributing to this new failure was the nation's new Constitution approved on October 5, 1988. The document provided numerous complex and costly social benefits, most covered by government spending. One article placed a limit of 12 percent on domestic annual real interest rates, which helped fuel inflationary expectations. Monthly price index rates went from 20 percent in August 1988 to 29 percent in December.

Public finances were hurt by the redistribution of tax revenues among federal, state, and local governments. The federal administration had to increase tax collection in order to transfer it to lower government levels, but it was not allowed to transfer expenditures of equivalent proportions.

By January 1989, as in all cases during the last five years, price pressures seemed to reach unmanageable levels.[9] During this month, the money supply soared by 50 percent. Expectations deteriorated to such an extent that government political stability appeared jeopardized. PMDB political supporters, business owners, and labor unions placed pressure on the government, calling for "stronger" measures.

Faced with a new deepening crisis, the authorities declared bank holidays for January 16 and 17 and announced the third "non-orthodox" experiment, called the Summer Plan.[10] This new diversion in economic policy, like the other two, resulted in the deterioration of the country's relationship with the international financial system. Table 8 shows the bad performance of domestic indicators. While the external sector improved in 1988, it gradually worsened in the first half of 1989.

Table 8
Brazil: Selected Economic Indicators

	1987	1988	1989
Public deficit (*) (operational) (as % of GDP)	5.7	4.8	6.9
Inflation GPI (in %) (*)	415.8	1037.6	1782.9
GDP growth (in %) (*)	2.9	-0.3	3.6
Trade balance (×) (billions US$)	8.911	19.100	161.42
International (×) reserves (Dec. 31) (billions US$)	7.458	9.140	9.679

Source: Central Bank of Brazil, Annual Reports.
(*) = "domestic" indicators.
(×) = external sector.
GPI = General Price Index

1989-1991: Reviving "Non-Orthodox" Experiments — Capital Outflows and Balance of Payments Crisis

The Summer Plan of January 1989 contained the same basic features of the other two recent experiments:

1. A price freeze on all goods and services.

2. A new monetary unit, the cruzado novo, equal to 1,000 cruzados.

3. The indexation through OTN (national treasury debt) was formally abandoned, as was the case with its predecessor, the ORTN (readjusted national treasury debt), abolished when the Cruzado Plan was announced.[11]

4. Provided exchange reserves fall below an unspecified level, a moratorium would again be placed on interest payments to foreign banks, as in February 1987. Debt-equity conversion auctions were also canceled from this time onward.

5. Measures were announced for the public sector, such as the dismissal of an unspecified number of civil servants and cuts in current expenditures and subsidies. These measures were never implemented, though, except for the decision to increase public sector prices and tariffs taken prior to the implementation of the price freeze.

The Summer Plan is now considered the worst experiment. It repeated the same mistakes of the two previous "plans": fighting inflation by trying to eliminate its consequences, instead of attacking its origins (the domestic macroeconomic disequilibrium, caused by the public deficit and excess spending in the private sector).

Only five months after the plan was initiated, it became clear that it had collapsed. Popular support for it vanished. Inflation was held to 4.2 percent in March and 5.2 percent in July, a level higher than the January rate of 36.6 percent, when the "Plan" was born. The authorities were forced to accept the reintroduction of indexation in June and created the National Treasury Bill (BTN) to replace the OTN. The return of high inflation rates was precipitated by a large adjustment in the minimum wage (70 percent) and the reindexation and upward trend in the consolidated public deficit, which reached 6.9 percent of GDP. (The nominal PSBR, however, jumped to 83.1 percent of GDP, against 53 percent in 1988 and 32.3 percent in 1987.)

The capital account of the balance of payments deteriorated due to reduced capital inflows,[12] a sharp drop in direct investments, and soaring capital flight. These results were also a consequence of a new moratorium on interest payments introduced in July 1989, after a sharp fall in international reserves.[13] All in all, the final result can be summarized through a quotation from the Central Bank Annual Report for 1989:

At the end of 1989, despite an international reserve level (US$7.3 billion in cash concept) which was practically equal to that of 1984 (US$7.5 billion), the country had US$4.6 billion in arrears, covering interest, profits, and other remittances not affected.

Since the inflow of new resources was insufficient, the country had to maintain a minimum level of cash reserves in the range of $7 billion, and this led to the concentration of foreign exchange in the Central Bank, as of July 1989 (moratorium).

In 1989, it was not possible to maintain the standby agreement with the IMF. As a result, the country did not receive the $795 million programmed for that year, and the commercial banks suspended disbursement of the final tranche of $600 million specified in the multiyear agreement dated September 22, 1988.

External debt auctions were suspended during 1989 as a result of the requirements of monetary policies. Informal payments of amortizations by companies with government participation were not allowed in 1989, since these amortizations were subjected to rescheduling according to the terms of the 1988 multiyear agreement.

In 1989, net capital movements registered a negative flow of $4.129 billion, in contrast to a net inflow of $2.921 billion in 1988. In the same year, the Brazilian external debt came to $114.7 billion, a growth of 1.1 percent over its 1988 position.

In short, the Central Bank reported a year of failures. On March 15, 1990, a new government took over, and a plan was immediately announced, known as Plano Collor.[14]

With the aim of combating high inflation rates, the government imposed a temporary, three-month wage and price freeze, followed by periodic adjustments according to forecast inflation rates. At the same time, because of the oversupply of fully indexed financial assets, it was determined by law that a substantial share of these assets would be made temporarily non-convertible to a "new" monetary unit — known as the cruzeiro — which was to have the same value as the "cruzado novo."

The retention of financial assets (about 60 percent of the stock on March 15) produced a broad and abrupt cutback in purchasing power and a substantial relief in the public internal debt, since a major proportion of the total assets was in public securities.

The compulsory debt reduction (the frozen stock was programmed to be convertible to cruzeiros in twelve months, starting in August 1991) produced a consequent reduction of interest payments, making it possible to diminish the government's financial outlays during the 18-month period.

This artificial gain, coupled with some gains in tax collection,[15] made it possible to close the government's accounts for the year with a small surplus. However, in 1991, the government's financial position again turned negative.

In an attempt to consolidate the reduction in inflationary expectations after some real liquidity growth in April, the government initiated a tight monetary policy in May based on very high interest rates.

Inflation did decline to acceptable levels (see Table 9) over time, but accelerated again in the last quarter. This upsurge was attributable to the policy of indexation, which was still being used.

External debt negotiations were supposed to be reinitiated in mid-October, when an "innovative" proposal was presented. The new idea was to transform the external debt owed to private banks into securities; at the same time, interest payments would be conditioned upon the availability of federal government fiscal resources (surplus). Since the moratorium of July 1989 was still in effect, the government also suggested that its interest in arrears (about $8 billion) be included in the amount of debt to be converted into securities. This new "Plan" was not considered seriously by the international financial system, which classified it as "non-starting."

It is important to take into consideration that President Fernando Collor's staff had been recruited from a group of old friends and young scholars who had no previous experience in public administration. Collor won the 1989 elections without any help from politicians and organized political groups. He succeeded in introducing himself as a young, modern, competent leader. Most of Collor's ideas were liberal in essence and market oriented in economics. Notwithstanding this overall orientation, the proposal for the debt negotiations had a clear populist appeal, as did the rhetoric used to support it. Negotiations collapsed before starting.

In May 1991, after a failed attempt at a "non-orthodox" stabilization plan,[16] Collor decided to change his economic team. Minister Zélia Cardoso de Mello was dismissed, along with all the staff of the Ministry of Economic Affairs, and replaced by the well-known conservative Ambassador Marcilio Marques Moreira.

Moreira began a process of gradual change in economic policies, based once again on conventional monetary and fiscal instruments. He also reinforced some structural reforms, such as the privatization of state enterprises, economic deregulation, and a gradual process of trade liberalization.

Moreira withdrew Zélia's proposal for the foreign debt and started negotiations with the IMF in order to get a standby program and institutional support for further debt negotiations. Discussion with the IMF lasted six months and ended with the approval of a Letter of Intent sent by the government to the IMF board on January 29, 1992.

The letter outlined a highly conventional stabilization program, based on a sharp reduction of the public deficit, a tight monetary policy, real adjustments in public tariffs, and international reserve increases through trade surpluses.

Moreira also succeeded in negotiating with the Paris Club, and he concluded negotiations with private banks concerning interest arrears. The moratorium had been over in September 1991. In March 1992, Moreira declared his intent to negotiate with private banks based on the guidelines set forth by the Brady Plan.

Table 9
Brazil: Selected Economic Indicators

	1990	1991	March 1992(b)
Inflation GPI *(in %)*	1500.0	480.0	430.0
GDP growth *(in %)*	-4.2	1.1	1.0-1.5
Investment rate *(in % of GDP)*	16.2	15.8	16.0
Trade balance *(in billions US$)*	10.990	10.972	15.500
International reserves *(Dec. 31) (in billions US$)*	9.973	10.500	10.500(a)

Source: Central Bank of Brazil, Annual Reports.
(a): Annual forecast, based on first quarter trends.
(b): Position on March 31, 1992.

SUMMING UP A DECADE:
LESSONS FROM CONFRONTATION EXPERIMENTS IN BRAZIL

G overnment responses to the debt problem in Brazil have been highly dependent on political support for domestic adjustments resulting from the lack of external financing.

During the 1982-1984 period, that support was provided by the military government in power. High social costs resulted in the defeat of the military in the 1984 elections. The PMDB opposition party took over and changed the rules toward "social" priorities: economic recovery, employment, social programs through government spending, and the gradual acceptance of the need for a debt moratorium. As a matter of fact, the PMDB economists openly favored "debt repudiation," arguing that debt service was the main source of Brazil's public deficit and an unimaginable drain of real resources to the developed world.

Since inflation and domestic disequilibrium remained, despite economic recovery, a series of "non-orthodox" or unconventional experiments in stabilization policies were undertaken, beginning in February 1986 with the

"Cruzado Plan." Continuing with the Bresser Plan in June 1987, the Summer Plan in January 1989, the Collor Plan I in March 1990, and Collor Plan II in February 1991, all have had the same final result: failure.

As to the debt question, all the plans offered the same response, that is, renegotiations aimed at reducing the service burden. Since the plans failed, in all cases the debt renegotiation proposals also collapsed. There is no way of knowing whether or not they could succeed by themselves. Clearly enough, however, the 1985-1991 period, with the exception of 1988, can be viewed as a "confrontation" phase: Brazil versus the international financial community. Apparently, the results have been poor enough to convince government authorities to change their priorities toward mutually acceptable terms — at least they were as of April 1992. Even without adequate political support, Collor and the majority of Brazilians seemed tired enough of inflation that they were ready to accept the necessary economic adjustment burden.

NOTES

1. Central Bank of Brazil. *Brazil - Economic Program, Internal and Adjustment,* February 1985.

2. The General Price Index (GPI) is the most accepted measure of inflation in Brazil, published by the Fundação Getúlio Vargas, Rio de Janeiro.

3. This concept, which excludes monetary and exchange corrections, was introduced by the IMF staff to analyze the government's efforts in reducing real expenditures and improving real receipts more accurately.

4. *Partido do Movimento Democrático Brasileiro,* a former political coalition of opposition parties.

5. As opposed to "orthodox" policies "recommended" by the IMF, essentially monetary and fiscal policies.

6. The Bresser Plan, in June 1987; the Summer Plan, in February 1989; the Collor Plan I, in March 1990; and the Collor Plan II, in February 1991.

7. The so-called "Plano Bresser," imposed by Finance Minister Bresser Pereira in June 1987, was a second version of the Cruzado Plan, based upon price controls and the elimination of all kinds of indexation. It lasted less than six months and so did the minister himself.

8. Wages were indexed by past inflation, which accelerated from 366 percent (Consumer Price Index) in 1987 to 933.6 percent in 1988.

9. General Price Index reached 36.6 percent, a level higher than the 26.6 percent of June 1987 (Plano Bresser) and the 17.8 percent of January 1986 (Plano Cruzado).

10. An analogy to the "Spring Plan" of Argentina, in September 1988.

11. OTN: *Obrigação do Tesouro Nacional,* Treasury bonds indexed to the General Price Index.
   ORTN: *Obrigação Reajustavel do Tesouro Nacional,* the old Treasury bond introduced for the first time in 1964, indexed also to the General Price Index.

12. The capital account of $4.179 billion was negative in 1989.

13. From the level of $10.5 billion in March 1989 to $8.5 billion in June.

14. The new president, Fernando Collor de Mello, named it "Plano Brasil Novo," but the Brazilian people referred to it as Plano Collor.

15. The government allowed tax payments in foreign "cruzados novos" during this time.

16. The so-called Plano Collor II was based on a price freeze and new rules for the domestic financial markets.

COMMENTS ON CHILE AND BRAZIL

Evan Tanner

It is by now a cliché that the 1980s were a "lost decade" for Latin countries. While growth stagnated, countries underwent difficult adjustments. The outstanding foreign debt also loomed large. Policymakers sought ways to ameliorate the effects of the "debt overhang." These policies involved varying degrees of market intervention. At the less interventionist extreme, some argued for a policy of "muddling through," while at the opposite end of the spectrum, some advocated large-scale debt forgiveness. In the middle are found a wide variety of plans instituted either unilaterally by countries or as a result of negotiation between creditor and debtor.

A fundamental question involves the effect of these policies on economic growth. How important were the debt strategies for renewed economic growth? What was the relationship between debt policy per se and other economic reforms? The cases of Chile and Brazil provide a good study in contrasts. The papers by Eric Haindl on Chile and Carlos Von Doellinger on Brazil highlight the role of debt policy in the overall macroeconomic and growth picture.

As Haindl notes, during the past decade, the Chilean economy has served as a model for its Latin American neighbors. In the wake of the debt crisis, Chile led the region in growth, investment, and macroeconomic stability. This happened for several reasons. Chile's leadership in trade liberalization was maintained throughout the period, as were fiscal and monetary discipline.

Nonetheless, at the onset of the debt crisis in the early 1980s, Chile suffered a severe recession and external payments problems, much like other countries in the region. In addition to trade and macro policies, the government pursued active strategies for foreign debt management. Much like other countries, Chile implemented mechanisms to facilitate debt repurchases, incentives for foreign investment, and facilities for debt-equity swaps.

Did these policies contribute to renewed economic growth? This question is pertinent, not only for Chile, but for other countries in the region as well. When one strips away the veil of technical formalities from debt policy, one finds a system of subsidies and incentives. From a pure efficiency standpoint, one has to ask what the welfare effects of such subsidies and incentives were. Unfortunately, there has been little assessment of the various debt mechanisms from an efficiency standpoint.

In this commentary, I will focus on two of the debt mechanisms discussed by Haindl, the debt-repurchase facility (Chapter XVIII) and the reinvestment mechanism (Chapter XIX).

Chapter XVIII addresses the problem of "debt overhang." A country's outstanding, non-performing debt was viewed as an impediment to investment and growth. Recently, this view has been disputed. For example, Warner (1992) suggests that the volume of external debt had little impact on investment rates in Latin America during the 1980s.[1] Rather, investment rates were similar to those that would have taken place, given the world movements in interest rates, income, and commodity prices.

Nonetheless, policies toward "debt overhang" were formulated throughout the 1980s. These plans ranged from interventionist to market based. In the middle were schemes such as the Bolivian and Mexican buy-back plans, which required some government intervention but involved the market as well. Chile's Chapter XVIII may be placed here.

A critical issue is how to measure the "benefits" of a Chapter XVIII transaction. There are two components to this issue. First, there is the benefit supposedly derived from the fact that the asset was purchased on the secondary market at a discount. Second, there is the issue of the exchange rate subsidy obtained by the domestic purchaser of the asset.

First, consider the fact that assets are purchased on the secondary market at a discount. Haindl suggests that the domestic purchaser benefits on the spread between the face and market values of the instrument. Thus, if the secondary market price of debt is 60 cents on the dollar, and an investor purchases instruments with a face value of $100, this investor has obtained a "gross benefit" of $40.

This may not be a correct way to measure "benefit." This benefit may accrue in accounting terms but not in economic terms. Presumably, the secondary market price reflects the market's perceived probability that the debt will, in fact, be serviced. The investor has paid $60 for an asset with a value the market places exactly at $60. The investor has to compare this purchase with other comparable purchases.

Consider next the exchange rate aspect of the transaction. During most of the period in which Chapter XVIII was important, the Chilean government pegged the exchange rate below its market clearing value. Absent Chapter XVIII, in order to repurchase debt, domestic investors had two options: Stand in a queue for dollars at the official rate or go to the parallel market. Chapter XVIII added a third option. A quota of foreign currency sales, at an exchange rate between the official and parallel rates, was set aside for debt repurchases. Investors benefit because the exchange rate is less than the parallel rate. This calculation abstracts from any rent-seeking behavior and ignores the shadow value of currency. At the same time, the government obtains revenue from the spread between the exchange rate for repurchases and the official rate.

Thus, abstracting from the rents dissipated to obtain a share of the quota, the government used the exchange rate to subsidize repurchases of foreign debt. Why was this desirable? From an efficiency standpoint, an economist is forced to ask questions such as, "Why subsidize this particular transaction?" and "Why subsidize it in this particular way?" Indeed, the most fundamental question is why the government chose to peg the exchange rate below its market clearing value.

A similar issue arises for Chapter XIX, a policy designed to induce foreign investors to keep their funds inside the country. The key element of this policy is, once again, an exchange rate subsidy. In return for keeping capital inside the country (for a minimum of four years), the foreign investor obtains access to dollars at the (artificially low) official exchange rate.

Of course, it is impossible to say that these policies were inefficient or "bad" without more closely examining the overall policy environment. These policies may have been second best, designed to counteract other distortions, particularly those that discourage investment.

It is ultimately impossible to evaluate policies such as Chapters XVIII and XIX without considering the broader macroeconomic policy environment. In order to stimulate investment, there must be a stable and competitive rate of return. This rate of return must incorporate both explicit taxes (i.e., capital gains taxes, corporation taxes, value added taxes) as well as implicit taxes (inflation, exchange depreciation, unstable regulatory environments).

It is in these latter categories that Chile distinguishes itself from its neighbors in the region. Many policies have made Chile a good place to invest. At the margin, mechanisms such as Chapters XVIII and XIX may have sweetened the deal. But the fundamental lesson from Chile was that such policies alone have ambiguous welfare effects and are not sufficient to cause economic renewal.

Von Doellinger's paper suggests that, while the Brazilian experience was very different from the Chilean one, it reinforces the main messages. First, debt mechanisms, in and of themselves, are of little help without a stable policy environment. To the degree that debt mechanisms help raise and stabilize the rate of return to investors, they will contribute to increased investment and growth. Good macro and trade policy makes debt mechanisms more effective, but the reverse does not appear to be true.

Von Doellinger reviews the sequence of failed plans in Brazil. Throughout the 1980s, starting with the Cruzado Plan, one sees a cycle of events: increasing inflation and budget deficits, followed by a package of ineffective policies. As a whole, these policies treated symptoms but not causes. Inflation was halted for a short time after the plan but soon returned stronger than ever.

The investment environment in Brazil tends to be uncertain. High and variable inflation, coupled with periodic defaults on domestic debt and highly unpredictable interest rate policies by the Central Bank make real interest rates unstable and highly variable. During some periods, real interest rates were extraordinarily high. This reflected the riskiness of government obligations. At other times, high and unexpected inflation caused the real interest rate to become highly negative. Indeed, inflation has served, over a long period, to be an effective way to tax financial assets. Over the period 1986 to 1991 (including the 1990 Collor Plan), inflation outstripped interest rates, causing the real return on government debt and other financial instruments to be negative. Such an environment does not encourage investment and long-term growth.

Against the backdrop of domestic policy was a series of policy initiatives regarding external debt. In March 1987, the Brazilians declared a moratorium on debt payments, but by 1988, they attempted to service debt once again. The negotiation process has dragged on well into the 1990s. Indeed, debt repudiation, an ideal long ago abandoned by most Latin countries, was still on the menu of options of the leading (though ultimately losing) candidate for president in the 1994 elections, Luis Ignacio (Lula) da Silva.

It is possible that money freed up from debt payments may ultimately increase investment. It is also possible, however, that savings from debt reduction will effectively expand the government's budget constraint, causing the public sector to increase rather than the private sector. Ultimately, Brazil requires a dramatic and profound adjustment of its public sector rather than the window-dressing economic plans of the past decade.

NOTE

1. Warner, A. 1992. "Did the Debt Crisis Cause Investment to Fall?" *Quarterly Journal of Economics.*

IV

PERU'S EFFORTS TO ACHIEVE REINSERTION IN THE INTERNATIONAL FINANCIAL SYSTEM

Humberto Campodónico

On July 28, 1990, when Alberto Fujimori was inaugurated as president of Peru, the Peruvian debt situation was among the most complex in the world. Peru's total medium- and long-term external indebtedness reached $20.341 billion, the equivalent of 80 percent of the gross domestic product (GDP). Annual debt servicing (repayment of principal plus interest) represented $2 billion, some 66 percent of all exports.

Since 1983, when the *Acción Popular* party governed under the leadership of Fernando Belaúnde Terry, a good part of this debt went unpaid and led to an accumulation of arrears. During the 1985-1990 period, arrears increased as a result of President Alan García's policy of allocating only 10 percent of total export earnings for payment of the external debt. Thus, as of July 1990, arrears totaled more than $13.472 billion; that is, 70 percent of the external debt was unpaid.

Considering the high level of arrears in payment of the external debt, the characteristics of the Peruvian case are exceptional. Even though the commercial debt arrears of other countries such as Argentina and Brazil have been higher in absolute terms, proportional to the size of other economies, the Peruvian arrears are larger (in regard to both commercial debt and total arrears). Since the Peruvian debt situation is in a class by itself, the study of the negotiations between Peru and its creditors is of the utmost importance.

During May-June 1990, before his inauguration, President-elect Fujimori studied a number of alternatives for confronting the debt problem. Finally, in August 1990, the government opted for the path of direct negotiations with the International Monetary Fund (IMF) and a strategy labeled "reinsertion in the international financial system," oriented toward an "integral solution" of the external debt problem.

This document analyzes the particular forms of "reinsertion" in the Peruvian case. First, a brief description of the state of the external debt and of projections regarding the balance of payments before the government began negotiations for reinsertion will be presented.

On April 5, 1992, an *autogolpe* (self-coup) took place, in which President Fujimori dissolved Congress and began a reorganization of the judiciary. The *autogolpe* was deplored by many countries and especially by the Organization of American States (OAS). The economic consequences of this political event were a suspension of outlays and credits committed by the Support Group, a suspension by the Inter-American Development Bank (IDB) of further credit agreements, and a "wait and see" attitude on the part of the IMF and the World Bank. Subsequently, elections were held to elect the Democratic Constituent Congress (October 1992) and municipal representatives (February 1993). These elections had a decisive impact on making the payment of arrears with the IMF and the World Bank (March 1993) viable and impacted new negotiations with the Paris Club (May 1993) as well.

In this manner, the Peruvian government's economic policy decisions regarding the negotiation of the external debt were influenced by political events; this factor complicates carrying out a purely economic analysis. Moreover, for reasons beyond the control of the author of this document, this analysis was written at different moments and periods. The first analysis covers the period from August 1990 to April 1992. This is followed by an analysis of the events of 1993, focusing principally on the "reinsertion" with the multilateral organizations, the May 1993 Paris Club negotiation, and the beginning of the negotiations with international private banks for the payment of arrears accumulated since 1983.

THE STABILIZATION PROGRAM OF AUGUST 1990

From the outset, the Fujimori government made contact with the IMF to put into effect a drastic macroeconomic stabilization program. One of the principal problems facing Peru at that time was hyperinflation (rising by 25 percent monthly), inherited from Alan García's government. Simultaneously, the government undertook a broad structural adjustment program, worked out in agreement with the World Bank, to stimulate the liberalization and deregulation of markets and prices and to remove the state from productive activity by privatizing state firms.

Payments were also resumed on current maturities with the multilateral agencies. Such payments had been made to the IMF since August 1989. In October and November 1990, payments of current maturities resumed with the World Bank and the IDB, without any negotiation involving Peru's "reinsertion."

Situation of the Peruvian External Debt

As of June 1991, Peru's total external debt registered $22.642 billion (see Table 1). Unlike in other Latin American countries, the medium- and long-term external public debt makes up the bulk of the external debt, some $20.975 billion or 93 percent of the total. The most important debt holders are the Paris Club, with $7.792 billion (34.4 percent); private commercial banks, with $5.860 billion (25.9 percent); the multilateral financial agencies (primarily the IMF, World Bank, and the IDB), with $3.671 billion (16.2 percent); and the Eastern European countries, with $1.446 billion (6.4 percent). Next in line, with smaller amounts, are the creditors without guaranteed loans, the Latin American countries,[1] and the medium- and long-term private debt, ending with the short-term debt of $1.413 billion (6.2 percent).

Table 1
Total External Debt as of June 30, 1991
(millions of US$)

		Total(1)	Arrears (1,2)
I.	Public (medium and long term)	20,975	14,913
	1. Multilateral	3,671	2,267
	a. IBRD (World Bank)	1,555	964
	b. IMF (3)	959	873
	c. IDB	1,101	428
	d. Others	56	2
	2. Paris Club	7,792	5,682
	3. Latin America	837	53
	4. Eastern Europe	1,446	110
	a. Russia	1,218	66
	b. Others	228	44
	5. Commercial banks	5,860	5,693
	6. Lenders of unsecured loans	1,369	1,108
II.	Private (medium and long term)	254	85
III.	Short term	1,413	0
IV.	Total	22,642	14,998

(1) Includes depreciation, interest, and moratorium interest.
(2) Included in the total of the previous column.
(3) Central Bank obligation.
Sources: Ministry of Economics and Finance and Central Reserve Bank.

Table 2
Balance of Payments: 1981-1990 (2)
(millions of US$)

	1981	1982	1983	1984	1985	1986	1987	1988	1989	1990(1)
I. Current account balance	-1,715	-1,534	-780	-132	198	-1,018	-1,466	-1,029	347	-665
A. Trade balance	-553	-429	293	1,007	1,172	-65	-521	-99	1,197	391
1. Exports FOB	3,249	3,293	3,015	3,147	2,978	2,531	2,661	2,691	3,488	3,276
2. Imports FOB	-3,802	-3,722	-2,722	-2,140	-1,806	-2,596	-3,182	-2,790	-2,291	-2,885
B. Financial services	-1,005	-958	-1,039	-1,076	-938	-760	-703	-765	-637	-693
1. Public sector	-456	-548	-636	-806	-707	-605	-538	-594	-483	-555
2. Private sector	-549	-410	-403	-270	-231	-155	-165	-171	-154	-138
C. Non-financial services	-318	-314	-253	-221	-170	-343	-422	-376	-448	-610
D. Transfer payments	161	167	219	158	134	150	180	211	235	247
II. Long-term capital	564	1,221	1,372	1,127	676	596	723	743	694	450
A. Public sector	305	989	1,431	1,392	814	606	679	718	637	470
1. Disbursements	1,620	1,934	1,530	1,026	693	495	585	350	380	245
2. Refinancing	80	109	1,024	499	201	0	0	0	699	0
a. Of depreciation	80	109	842	418	182	0	0	0	615	0
b. Of interest	0	0	182	81	19	0	0	0	84	0
3. Depreciation	-1,394	-1,054	-1,145	-1,441	-1,329	-1,453	-1,591	-1,492	-1,206	-1,143
4. Other capital	-1	0	22	1,308	1,249	1,564	1,685	1,860	764	1,368
B. Private sector	259	232	-59	-265	-138	-10	44	25	57	-20
III. Net basic balance (I + II)	-1,151	-313	592	995	874	-422	-743	-286	1,041	-215
A. Short-term capital and errors and omissions	647	437	-632	-748	-594	-95	-42	-112	-178	361
IV. Balance of payments (III + IIIA)	-504	124	-40	247	280	-517	-785	-398	863	146

(1) Preliminary.   (2) Excludes financial cost of unpaid services.

By June 1991 (again, see Table 1), arrears rose to $14.998 billion, that is, 66.2 percent of the total external debt. The most important arrears were with the following creditors:

1. Private commercial banks owned $5.693 billion, the equivalent of 38 percent of all arrears. Note that the arrears with the private banks are equivalent to 97.2 percent of the total owed to these institutions.

2. The Paris Club, with $5.682 billion, owned some 37.9 percent of all arrears. As in the preceding case, arrears account for a significant amount (73 percent) of the total owed to the Paris Club.

3. The multilateral agencies, with $2.267 billion, owned the equivalent of 15.1 percent of the total arrears. Here, arrears with the IMF and the World Bank are the most important.

4. The rest of the creditors' arrears are less significant, except for those with lenders of unbacked credit. Though these arrears account for only 7.4 percent of all arrears, they constitute 81 percent of the total owed to these providers.

There are no arrears on the short-term external debt. It should be noted, however, that the principal is not being repaid; only interest payments are being met. To carry out the "reinsertion" of Peru in the manner proposed by the government, it was first necessary to settle the arrears problem with the multilateral agencies and to reschedule the debt with the Paris Club.

YEARLY DEBT SERVICING AND ITS IMPACT ON THE BALANCE OF PAYMENTS

The annual servicing of the external debt (repayment of principal plus interest) rises by nearly $2 billion annually, as can be seen in the balance of payments for 1981-1990 (see Table 2). Of this amount, close to $1.4 billion goes toward repaying the principal, while the rest covers interest. Since the value of exports on average is only $3 billion, servicing the external debt corresponds to 66 percent of exports, an amount greater than the Latin American average.

This indicates that the volume of exports did not even allow a resolution of the problem of current payments on Peru's external debt. Peru's challenge was not only to resume payment of current maturities but also to pay its arrears on the external debt, which, as shown, rose to $15 billion. The mere mention of this figure indicates the magnitude of the problem.

THE BLUEPRINT FOR "REINSERTION"

According to the agreement with the IMF, the plan being laid out was to resolve fully the problem of the external debt. Presented during negotiations between the Peruvian government and the IMF (see Table 3), this plan required nearly $18.5 billion of financing for the years 1991 and 1992 (see line 6, Table 3). Of this amount, $13.5 billion (see line 3) corresponded to arrears with the Paris Club, private banks, and the multilateral agencies, while $5.2 billion (see line 2) corresponded to current obligations on servicing the external debt. To finance these proposed payments, the plan called for a rescheduling of the debt with the Paris Club and the deferral of payments to the private international banks, which totaled $14.4 billion during 1991 and 1992.

Table 3
External Financing Requirements for the Economic Program and Solving the External Debt
(in billions of US$)

Financing required	1991	1992	Total
1. Current account deficit	0.2	0.3	0.5
2. Public sector debt service (multilateral)	2.6	2.6	5.2
3. Total arrears	11.7	1.8	13.5
4. Change in gross reserves	0.1	0.2	0.3
Minus:			
5. Disbursements of loans contracted and private capital flows	0.4	0.7	1.1
6. Financing required (1+2+3+4-5)	14.2	4.2	18.4
Sources of financing			
7. Rescheduling, deferment, and relief of bilateral and private debt	13.1	1.3	14.4
8. Requirements to finance the regularization of the debt with multilateral creditors	0.6	2.1	2.7
– Disbursements from multilateral creditors	0.4	1.9	2.3
– FLAR (Latin American Reserve Fund)	0.2	0.2	0.4
9. Additional official financing required	0.5	0.8	1.3
10. Total sources of financing (7+8+9)	14.2	4.2	18.4

Note: It is assumed that arrears with the IDB will be paid toward the end of 1991 and that the IMF and the World Bank will implement the Accumulation of Rights and Shadow Adjustment Programs, respectively. Arrears will be paid off toward the end of 1992.
Source: World Bank 1991b, Annex 2.

With respect to the multilateral agencies, novel mechanisms were proposed to regularize arrears with the IMF and the World Bank. Debt refinancing equivalent to $1.8 billion would be realized in 1992 (see Table 3, line 8). As for the IDB, there would be an immediate settlement since the size of these arrears was much smaller ($430 million).

Nevertheless, a financing gap of $1.3 billion remained (see line 9, Table 3). It was proposed that a support group be formed to lend Peru the amount necessary to stabilize its balance of payments.

From 1993 onward, financing needs became more difficult because the volume of debt servicing increased significantly (see Table 6). However, the main strategic problem of "reinsertion" involved the arrears accumulated with multilateral agencies during the 1991-1992 period. Below, the approaches to the period 1993-1999 will be studied.

THE NEGOTIATION OF THE "REINSERTION"

During March-April 1991, negotiations produced an agreement on a proposal for reinsertion. The reinsertion process was to be fulfilled in five stages:

1. The formation of a Support Group[2] that will contribute the amounts needed to finance balance of payments needs that cannot be covered by the following points;
2. The signing of a Reference Program with the IMF[3] for the period 1991-1992;
3. The implementation of special mechanisms for paying arrears with the IMF and the World Bank, the payment of arrears with the IDB, and continued payments on current maturities with these agencies;
4. The rescheduling of official bilateral debt with the Paris Club; and
5. The continuation of deferred payments on existing debt arrears with the international commercial banks.

Below, these steps are analyzed in detail.

Formation of the Support Group

The Support Group was formed after meetings held in April and June 1991.[4] On September 9, 1991, the final meeting of the Support Group took place in Washington, D.C., at which point commitments were obtained for about $1.152 billion from eleven countries (see Table 4). The principal contributors were Japan and the United States, with $420 and $406 million, respectively, accounting for some 72 percent of the total. Contributions from the other countries were less significant, but Germany stood out, providing $136 million. Fifty-four percent of the $1.152 billion took the form of concessional loans, and the balance consisted of donations.

Table 4
Contributions from the Support Group: 1991-1992
(millions of US$)

Country	Amount Agreed to	Disbursement Received	In-Cash Support	Form of	Local Currency (1)
1. Japan	420	315	Yes	Loan	Yes
2. United States	406(2)	20	Both	Donation	Yes
3. France	26(3)	16	Both	Donation	No
4. Holland	23	12	Yes	Donation	No
5. Switzerland	10	10	Yes	Donation	Yes
6. Italy	15	0	Yes	Donation	No
7. Canada	53(4)	0	No	Donation	Yes
8. Germany(3)	136(5)	0	Both	Loan	Yes
9. Spain	55	0	Yes	Loan	Not defined
10. Sweden	5	0	Yes	Donation	Not defined
11. Belgium	3	0	Yes	Donation	Not defined
Total	**1,152**	**373**			

Form of payment		
Loan	621	315
Donation	531	58

Form of disbursement		
Cash	690	373
Stocks and bonds	462	0

(1) Disbursements must have a countervalue in local currency.
(2) $155 million in cash, of which $50 million has been contracted.
(3) $10 million is a loan in machinery.
(4) $40 million in machinery and $13 million in foodstuffs.
(5) $30 million is cash to finance imports.
Sources: Ministry of Economics and Finance and Central Reserve Bank.

The formation of this Support Group was an indispensable requisite for approval of the 1991-1992 Economic Program by the IMF Executive Board and for renegotiating the bilateral debt with the Paris Club.

According to one government official, The resources should be disbursed in cash or for projects contained in the budget that can be rapidly executed; otherwise, the Treasury will not enjoy effective relief to pay its external debt. Similarly, they should be in addition

to existing bilateral programs of cooperation and consist of donations or loans given on extremely concessional terms. In this
manner, these resources would allow for an important improvement
in the medium-term profile of external debt servicing.(Valdivia-
Velarde, Ugarteche, and Portocarrero 1992, 22)

Negotiations with the IMF and the World Bank

Initially, it was thought that the arrears problem could be resolved
through the arrangement of a "bridge loan" granted by a group of countries,
including the principal debt-holding countries and some Latin American
governments. In this manner, two goals would be fulfilled simultaneously. On
the one hand, the arrears would be straightened out, and on the other, as a
consequence, fresh credit could be obtained from the IMF and the World
Bank. This would make it possible to "alleviate" the social costs of the
stabilization and structural adjustment program.

Nevertheless, the strategy of arranging a "bridge loan" was watered down
soon after the stabilization package was launched on August 8, 1990. The
government faced a major problem: Unlike other countries that had used this
mechanism to "clean up" their arrears with the multilateral agencies (consider
the cases of Guyana, Honduras, Zambia, among others), the extraordinarily
high volume of Peruvian arrears made it difficult to obtain a "bridge loan" from
the different governments. In the case of the IMF, Peru owed SDR 625 million
(the equivalent of $873 million) on June 30, 1991. This represented 25 percent
of the total arrears of all countries working with the IMF.

As for the World Bank, on June 30, 1991, the arrears on principal and
interest payments of all countries totaled $1.782 billion, of which $855.9
million (48 percent of the total owed) was owed by Peru. As a result, the
"bridge loan" needed to solve Peru's arrears problem amounted to nearly
$1.728 billion, which was considered impossible to obtain.

For this reason, the IMF and the World Bank proposed ad hoc
approaches to solving the arrears problem. In the case of the IMF, the
approach known as "accumulation of rights" was proposed:

The rights approach...provides that members can earn rights toward
future financing from the Fund through the implementation of a
comprehensive economic program with macroeconomic and structural policy standards associated with programs supported by
extended and ESAF [Economic Stabilization and Adjustment Fund]
arrangements....Under the rights approach, the encashment of
accumulated rights would take place after the clearance of arrears
to the Fund as the first disbursement under a successor financial
arrangement (for example, under the EFF [Extended Financing

Facility] or ESAF) approved by the Fund, once all requirements for such a successor arrangement have been met. (International Monetary Fund 1991, 70)

In the case of the World Bank, there was no specific plan for solving the issue of payment by countries with prolonged arrears. To settle the Peruvian case, the World Bank implemented a new approach, which was adopted by its Board in May 1991:

> In the past few months, in response to requests from the Peruvian government, the international community has searched for the structure of a financing plan for Peru. This plan would involve a coordinated effort by the most important bilateral donors and the three international financial institutions (IFIs), which would seek to eliminate Peru's interest arrears, to reprogram a part of the bilateral debt, and to provide new money. In this context, on May 2, 1991, the Board of the World Bank agreed on a new thrust for supporting programs to resolve debt problems of countries with major arrears that are implementing substantial and sustained economic policy reforms, as in the case of Peru. (World Bank 1991c, 1)

This approach[5] proposes the following:

> The country would establish a track record on adjustment measures over the preclearance performance period. During the period, the IBRD [International Bank for Reconstruction and Development] would develop and process loans, but would not sign them, make them effective, or disburse any funds against them. After the performance period is over, and following the clearance of arrears, the country would receive disbursements on loans approved during the performance period, as well as on previous loans that had been suspended....During the performance period, a support group of other lenders or donors would be essential to provide sufficient funding to support the needs of the economy and facilitate the country's servicing of debt outstanding to the IBRD and the IMF. (World Bank 1991b, 73-74)

In a strict sense, the IMF and World Bank approach implies a deferred (non-immediate) refinancing of the arrears of the debtor country. The amounts needed to pay the arrears would accumulate in IMF and World Bank accounts during a specified period (in the Peruvian case, the period 1991-1992). If the country fulfills the goals of the IMF Reference Program and the Structural Adjustment Program, then it will become a debt holder of the disbursements of these agencies, upon the payment of arrears with a "bridge loan."

Concretely, in regard to Peru, this meant:

1. On September 12, 1991, as part of the Reference Program, the IMF approved a Rights Accumulation Program (RAP) to support Peru's stabilization program. If the goals of the macroeconomic program were met, this arrangement would allow Peru to accumulate "rights" that would lead to a disbursement by the IMF, following a clean-up of arrears. At the end of the arrangement, the remaining arrears could be canceled with a bridge loan that could be paid off with the IMF disbursement after the settlement of arrears. The total arrears accumulated during the arrangement, which equal the sum total of arrears, rise to 625 SDR.

2. Provisions from the World Bank granted three Structural Adjustment Loans (SAL) in the amount of $900 million:

The World Bank will authorize a loan to Peru for Commercial Reform, a loan for Structural Adjustment, and a loan for reforms of the financial sector. The loans would total $900 million, which would normally be within the range of available lending to Peru if it did not have the problem of arrears. Each loan would be subjected to approval by the Board, but would not be signed nor would it become effective until the arrears are cleared up. After the approval of the Board, there would be a regular and permanent monitoring on the progress of the reforms, which would be reported to the Board. (World Bank 1991c, 9-10)

Arrears with the IDB

The arrears with the IDB were less significant than the arrears with the IMF and the World Bank, reaching $433 million in September 1991. In this case, a bridge loan from the Latin American Reserve Fund (FLAR) was obtained in the amount of $325 million. This allowed Peru to pay its arrears to the IDB on September 13, 1991. An adjustment loan for the commercial sector was arranged in the amount of $425 million (September 18), and $325 million was disbursed immediately. Other planned IDB loans to Peru include loans in the areas of electricity, health, sanitation, and roads; these total $1.1 billion.

The Negotiations with the Paris Club

The negotiations with the Paris Club took place on September 17, 1991. Peru obtained debt relief from the Paris Club debt holders on their current maturities for the 1991-1992 period, agreeing to the payment of $340 million instead of the $850 million originally anticipated.

With regard to the amount of external debt unpaid since 1983 ($6.545 billion), the government negotiated a debt rescheduling whose terms are as follows (see Table 5):

1. The rescheduling of $4.714 billion of arrears (principal and interest) on September 30, 1991, and the rescheduling of the current maturities for October 1991 through December 1992 ($290 million) of the debt contracted prior to the cut-off date.[6] This pre-cut-off date debt was rescheduled under the Terms of Houston for official concessional loans, which are to be paid in twenty years with a ten-year grace period. Officially backed commercial loans are to be repaid in fifteen years with an eight-year grace period.

2. The rescheduling of the $467 million that corresponded to the interest that accrued from consolidating the debt contracted prior to the cut-off date. Of this amount, 70 percent ($327 million) will be paid from 1995 to 1997, while the remainder ($140 million) will be paid from 1992 to 1994.

3. The rescheduling of the arrears (principal and interest) held on September 30, 1991, on the debt contracted after the cut-off date ($1.036 billion). These arrears will be paid over six years beginning in June 1993.

4. A new meeting of the Paris Club (to be held at the beginning of 1993) to reschedule the servicing of the pre-cut-off date debt that expires beginning in 1993.

Table 5
Paris Club - Total Relief Obtained
(millions of US$)

	1991-1992
I. Pre-cut-off date public debt (1)	5,449
Arrears as of September 30, 1991	4,714
Maturities (2)	290
Rescheduled interest (3)	327
Deferment of interest (4)	118
II. Post-cut-off date public debt (5)	1,036
III. Private debt (6)	60
IV. Total relief (I+II+III)	6,545

(1) Credits contracted through 1982.
(2) From October 1, 1991, through December 31, 1992.
(3) 70% of the interest of rescheduled pre-cut-off date arrears and maturities.
(4) 30% of the interest of rescheduled pre-cut-off date arrears and maturities.
(5) Credits contracted since 1983.
(6) Not secured by the Peruvian public sector and deposited in the Central Reserve Bank as of September 30, 1991.
Sources: Ministry of Economics and Finance and Central Reserve Bank.

The government's principal objective in this rescheduling was to minimize the pressure of payments for the 1991-1992 period. This objective was achieved. The schedule for payments from 1993 onward is considered difficult. However, this was not seen as problematic; new debt renegotiations were to occur during the first months of 1993 (these did, in fact, take place in May 1993).

The Continuation of the Moratorium with the Private Banks

The external debt with international private banks approaches $5.860 billion (of which 97 percent is in arrears). As a result, the value of Peruvian external debt titles on the secondary market reached levels of 4.25 percent in December 1990. Following the September 1991 rescheduling, their value rose to 12.5 percent. In March 1992, their price was 14.5 percent (*Latin Finance* 1992, 9).

Toward the end of 1991, the Peruvian government clearly established the position that the country could neither pay the arrears nor resume payments of current maturities on this debt. As a result, "in March 1991, Peru recommenced contacts with the Steering Committee of the commercial banks, led by Citibank, with the goal of achieving a realistic and joint solution with this credit source" (Valdivia Velarde, Ugarteche, and Portocarrero 1992, 28). Both the IMF and the World Bank agree that during 1991 and 1992, Peru cannot resume service payments on its debt with the commercial banks.

> Unless an agreement could be reached which did not include payments in cash, the arrears on these loans will continue to grow during the period. After the legal proceedings brought by the commercial banks against Peru in 1989-1990, the government negotiated an agreement with them in which it agreed to forego the provisions of the Statute of Limitations, if the banks suspended the bankruptcy proceedings initiated in February of 1990. (World Bank 1992, 23)

As of April 1992, no defined policy for settling the problem of the commercial banks had been announced. Later, as shown below, the Peruvian government began negotiations with the commercial banks to swap external debt titles as part of the process of privatizing state firms.

The Other Debt Holders

The Peruvian government also decided to reschedule its debt with the Latin American countries. Up until 1991, this debt was paid automatically through the Asociación Latinoamericana de Integración (ALADI) Arrangement of Payments and Reciprocal Credits. As of the end of 1993, however, service payments were regularly being fulfilled.

As for the debt owed to Eastern European countries (80 percent of which corresponds to Russia), the Peruvian government suspended terms of payment in kind which had been made since the previous decade. According to the government, this was done because, even though this form of debt payment did not imply an outflow of foreign exchange, it did represent strong pressure on the treasury insofar as Peruvian entrepreneurs selling to these countries had to be paid. A different form of payment is being studied; in the meantime, payments remain suspended.

Payments on the external debt to non-backed debt holders remain suspended. According to the government, formulas are being studied to resume these payments.

BALANCE OF PAYMENTS PROJECTIONS AFTER THE SEPTEMBER 1991 NEGOTIATIONS

1991-1992 Period

According to IMF and World Bank estimates, as a result of Peru's negotiations with its debt holders, the balance of payments during the period 1991-1992 is projected to be as follows:

1. The gross external financing required for the period 1991-1992 will reach $20.7 billion (see line 5, Table 5). This estimate incorporates the expected levels of increase in international reserves and support for the nonfinancial current account deficit.

Once the disbursements of arranged loans are taken into account, the financing needs are reduced to $18.8 billion. The bulk of the requirements are related to financing the arrears ($13.855 billion). The rest has to do with servicing the public sector external debt, which rises to $2.616 and $2.398 billion, respectively, for 1991 and 1992. It should also be noted that debt servicing will be equivalent to approximately 80 percent of Peru's annual exports of goods.

2. The sources of financing for these $18.8 billion are as follows:

- Line 11 refers to the debt rescheduling with the Paris Club and the deferral on arrears payments ("rollover") to the private banks. This amounts to $15.065 billion for the period 1991-1992.

- Line 12 refers to additional disbursements by the multilateral agencies. These add up to $3.681 billion in 1991-1992.

- In 1991, the most important disbursements ($654 million) were provided by the IDB and the Latin American Reserve Fund (LARF) in accordance with the agreements contained in the Accumulation of Rights Program (IMF) and in the Shadow Loans (World Bank), which specify that neither the IMF nor the World Bank will disburse loans.

- In 1992, disbursements by the IDB and the LARF are taken into account. However, the most important disbursements correspond to the IMF and the World Bank, since a clearing of the arrears ($1.728 billion) with these agencies will be realized.

- Line 13 refers to the financing needs to be provided by the Support Group. These are estimated to be $700 million. As shown previously, the Support Group promised credits totaling $1.1 billion, with which the requirements would be satisfied.

1993-1999 Period

The external financing required for the period 1993-1999 varies between $2.6 and $3.3 billion annually (see, again, Table 6). These estimates are based on macroeconomic projections made by the Peruvian government, along with IMF and World Bank teams.[7] According to this scenario, Peru will continue to run current accounts deficits until 1996, with a projected surplus beginning in 1997 (see line 10, Table 6).

The payment of the external debt will fluctuate between $2.5 and $3.6 billion per year. These servicing figures take into account the new amounts arising from loans agreed to and to be arranged during the period.

It is assumed that foreign investment (line 7) will fluctuate between $200 and $500 million per year. The financial resources to cover balance of payments requirements during the 1993-1999 period will come primarily from increased financial flows from the multilateral agencies and the governments of the Paris Club (see line 12). Additionally, it is assumed that the Peruvian government will continue to reschedule debt servicing with the international commercial banks, the volume of which will vary each year between $0.7 and $1.1 billion during the period (see lines 2 and 11, Table 6). In other words, no payments to the private banks[8] are foreseen during 1993-1999.

Under these conditions, a financial gap of $200 to $500 million per year (line 13) is expected. This could be covered in a number of ways: increased loans from the IMF, debt reduction schemes, improvements in the trade balance, and new credits from the Support Group, among others.

Recent Developments in the Peruvian External Debt Negotiations

Payment of Arrears to the IMF and the World Bank

In March 1993, the Peruvian government managed to pay the arrears to the IMF through the fulfillment of a Rights Accumulation Program. An Extended Fund Facility (EFF) arrangement was signed for a period of three years (through March 1996) in the amount of $1.33 billion, of which $870

Table 6
Peru: Projected Balance of Payments, 1991-1999

	1991	1992	1993	1994	1995	1996	1997	1998	1999
Financing Required									
1. Current account deficit	536	492	465	366	236	88	-63	-72	-137
2. Public sector debt service									
- Debentures	2616	2398	2494	2635	2727	2890	3192	3406	3642
- Multilateral	513	530	625	688	708	749	889	933	987
- Bilateral	1208	1170	1128	1170	1193	1252	1341	1434	1533
- Private	895	698	741	777	826	889	962	1039	1122
3. Outstanding arrears									
- Current year	12055	1800	0	0	0	0	0	0	0
- Multilateral	379	1800	0	0	0	0	0	0	0
- Bilateral	5322	0	0	0	0	0	0	0	0
- Private	6354	0	0	0	0	0	0	0	0
4. Change in gross reserves	454	303	223	225	200	198	100	100	122
5. Gross financing required (1+2+3+4)	15661	4993	3182	3226	3163	3176	3229	3434	3627
6. Disbursements of loans contracted	255	200	80	68	51	3	0	0	0
7. Private capital flows	908	545	509	654	727	844	731	186	291
8. Increase in arrears	0	0	0	0	0	0	0	0	0
9. Other debentures and adjustments	0	0	0	0	0	0	0	0	0
10. Financing required (5-6-7-8-9)	14498	4248	2593	2504	2385	2329	2498	3248	3336
Sources of Financing									
11. Rescheduling and deferment of debt	13598	1467	743	798	736	785	854	1041	1296
- Bilateral	6352	769	2	21	-90	-102	-108	2	174
- Private	7246	698	741	777	826	887	962	1039	1122
12. Additional disbursements	900	2781	1337	1466	1373	1324	1549	1612	1675
- Multilateral	654	2328	502	624	505	449	665	692	719
- LARF (Latin American Reserve Fund)	484	200	0	0	0	0	0	0	0
- IMF, IDB, World Bank	170	2128	502	624	505	449	665	692	719
- Bilateral	246	453	835	844	868	875	884	920	956
13. Additional financing needed	0	0	514	237	276	220	95	595	565
14. Total sources of financing (11+12+13)	14498	4248	2594	2503	2385	2329	2498	3248	3336

Source: World Bank 1992, 46.

million was committed to canceling arrears. The rest of the credit still has not been disbursed.

Also in March 1993, the arrears to the World Bank were paid through the approval of three "Shadow Loans" signed during 1992. These included a $300 million loan for the commercial sector, $300 million in structural adjustment lending, and a $400 million adjustment loan for the financial sector, for a total of $1 billion. Of this amount, $867 million has been disbursed to pay the arrears. The rest of the credit remains to be disbursed.

Negotiation with the Paris Club

At the beginning of May 1993, a second set of negotiations took place between the Peruvian government and the Paris Club. The goal of these negotiations was to reschedule the current maturities coming due between January 1, 1993, and March 31, 1996. Their volume reached $3.109 billion.

The principal accomplishment of these negotiations was obtaining $1.896 billion in debt relief for the period. This reduced the pressure of payments by over 60 percent. Thus, payments during this period reached $1.213 billion, split up in the following manner: $415 million in 1993, $374 million in 1994, and $424 million in 1995.

The arrangement with the Paris Club holds for the same period of time as the Extended Fund Facility agreement with the IMF. Furthermore, the Paris Club agreed to alleviate the interest from the 1991 rescheduling (despite the express prohibition contained in the 1991 agreement against their renegotiation in future agreements). This resulted in relief of $335 million for the triennium.

Net Flow with the Multilateral Agencies and the Paris Club

For the period August 1990 through August 1993, the net flow of foreign exchange (actual outlays minus repayments and interest) yields a negative $41.171 billion (see Table 7). It is worth pointing out that these amounts were negative with the IMF ($499 million), the World Bank ($469 million), and the IDB ($403 million) but were positive with the Paris Club ($200 million).

Negotiations with the Private Banks

The Peruvian government is trying to reach an agreement to settle its arrears (which amount to nearly $6 billion) with the private international banks. In November 1992, by Decree Law 25848 (November 23, 1992), the government approved an agreement made in its negotiations with the international banks to suspend the period of tolling the external debt [charging additional fees on arrears]. Recently, in November 1993, the time limit on the "Tolling Agreement" was extended until February 15, 1994.

Table 7
Costs of the Reinsertion 1990-1993
(millions of US$)

I. Disbursements	
- IDB disbursements	558
- World Bank disbursements	1017
- IMF disbursements	870
- Paris Club disbursements	602
Total	3047
II. Payments made by Peru	
- Paid to IDB	961
- Paid to World Bank	1486
- Paid to IMF	1369
- Paid to Paris Club	402
Total	4218
III. Net flow (II-I)	-1171

Sources: World Bank, IMF, IDB, Central Reserve Bank of Peru.

The official framework for arriving at a comprehensive solution to the external debt with the international banks consists of the negotiation of a "Brady Plan." Peru is one of the fifteen countries included in this strategy, which was announced by the U.S. Secretary of the Treasury, Nicholas Brady. The Peruvian government has announced that on September 11, 1994, it will begin negotiations on the Brady Plan. As yet, no details are known, nor is there a list of choices that will be offered to the banks.

However, apart from the Brady Plan, the Peruvian government is willing to allow external debt to be used in the program begun in 1992 to privatize state firms. Thus, in November 1993, the Peruvian government promulgated Law 26,250, which allows swaps of private bank loans for the purchase of public firms. Among other precepts, the law establishes that "the contribution in cash will not be less than 10 percent of the base price" and that the percentage of payment that will be accepted in external debt instruments will be established in each case by the Comisión de Promoción de Inversion Privada (Commission for the Promotion of Private Investment, COPRI).

Presently, the negotiations with the private banks continue. The government wants to arrive at an agreement so that external debt can be used to purchase a number of firms beginning in March 1994. There are still various problems that must be solved before these negotiations can prosper, however; the first concerns the impasse with the Steering Committee of creditor banks (led by Citibank) over a debt with Chemical Bank and American Express which had been canceled by the Peruvian government in 1986. The Steering Committee demands that this debt be recognized again by the Peruvian government as a necessary first step toward any agreement leading to debt swaps for state firms.

This debt was incurred in 1981-1982 by the Peruvian Steamship Company (Compañia Peruana de Vapores) — a state firm — for the purchase of two ships, the *Mantaro* and the *Pachitea*. In 1983, this debt was backed by the Peruvian state. Nevertheless, it was later called into question because, according to the Peruvian government, a number of offenses had been committed, of which Chemical Bank was aware. In 1986, the Congress canceled the debt by promulgating a legislative decree. The debt has since risen to $72 million (including interest unpaid and in arrears). Presently, a commission of the Democratic Constituent Congress has initiated proceedings to investigate the case.

On the other hand, broad sectors of Peruvian public opinion propose that a Brady Plan first be agreed upon. Then within the framework of such an agreement, debt swaps would be initiated for public enterprises. Proponents of this position maintain that the proceeds from swapping the external debt for state firms will effect only very small amounts ($300-$400 million) of the total debt ($6 billion); therefore, they argue that this plan would not result in an integral solution to the debt with the commercial banks. Similarly, the multilateral agencies, including the IMF, also see the negotiation of a Brady Plan as the central strategy for fully resolving the external debt with the creditor banks.

In the author's view, the following steps should be taken to fulfill negotiations with the private banks:

- Resolve the dispute over the debt with Chemical Bank and American Express.

- Negotiate a Brady Plan that includes a full solution to the problem of the external debt with the private banks. Full solutions should be sought rather than options that, in practice, only amount to refinancing or advance payments. The Peruvian government must announce that there will be no other mechanism for swapping debt for state assets except the Brady Plan. Such an announcement would cause the price of the external debt to return to its real level, that is, to a price that reflects Peru's real capacity for payment.

- Set the country's capacity for payment in accordance with economic goals for reactivation and growth. The country has suffered severe depression since 1988, with the 1992 GDP at a level 27 percent lower than the 1988 GDP. This translates into a high social cost for the poorest strata of the population. In 1993, the GDP grew 6.5 percent, and the Central Reserve Bank projects additional growth of 4.5 percent in 1994, a goal which seems modest and must be maintained.

If the deficit that needs to be financed by the central government is considered (excluding payments to private banks), the deficit climbs to 2.56 and 2.58 percent of the respective GDPs for 1993 and 1994 (see Table 8). This deficit, in agreement with the IMF, will be financed almost wholly by borrowing abroad since the internal tax base — although it has improved over the last two years — hardly exceeds 10 percent of the GDP. Similarly, the official position is that it is neither possible nor desirable to obtain further credits to finance additional payments on the external debt.

Table 8
Operations of Non-financial Public Sector
(% of GDP)

	1992	1993	1994
I. Central government current account	-0.34	-0.41	-0.39
II. Other public sector current account	0.99	0.96	0.91
III. Total government current account (I+II)	0.65	0.55	0.52
IV. Privatization revenues	0.12	0.44	1.03
V. Capital expenses	3.49	3.55	4.13
VI. Economic results (III+IV+V)	-2.72	-2.56	-2.58
VII. Public sector financing requirements	2.72	2.56	2.58
- External financing	1.86	2.58	2.58
- Internal financing	0.86	-0.02	0.00

Source: Peru's Central Bank, 1993.

For this reason, the author concurs with the following claim made by Oscar Hendrick, an official at the Central Reserve Bank: "Further pressures upon our internal and external accounts cannot be created. The fiscal and balance of payments constraints facing the country reinforce this position. It is estimated that during the 1993-1995 period, the deficit that the central government will have to finance will reach $1.344 billion. This amount will increase in the event that some solution is attempted with the creditor banks"(Hendrick and Pereda 1993, 38).

On the other hand, the economist Carlos Paredes maintains, "first there should be negotiations according to the country's capacity to pay. The negotiation should be guided by specific quantitative goals for forgiving debt, including the principal as well as interest. These goals should be drawn from a serious and detailed analysis of the ability to sustain debt servicing under different scenarios, in other words, an exercise in solvency" (Paredes 1993, 28).

Along these lines, when analyzing the balance of payments current account deficit for 1993 and 1994, the Central Reserve Bank calculates that this will oscillate around $2.5 billion, an amount which is presently being financed by the short-term inflow of capital. This is being attracted by the interest differential between the rates paid in Peru and the principal international capital markets. On the other hand, the Central Reserve Bank projects that payments on the external debt will rise to $2.344 and $2.944 billion in 1993 and 1994, respectively. Of these amounts, the actual payments to be made will fluctuate around $1 billion. This is equivalent to 30 percent of all exports, a very high percentage.

For all these reasons, the most sensible and advantageous approach for the country is to negotiate a Brady Plan that comprehensively settles the external debt arrears with the private banks.

Table 9
Summary of Balance of Payments: 1992-1994 (1)
(millions of US$)

	1992	1993	1994
Current account balance	-2,477	-2,576	-2,499
A. Trade balance	-567	-539	-569
1. Exports FOB	3,484	3,383	3,508
2. Imports FOB	-4,051	-3,922	-4,077
B. Financial services	-1,358	-1,472	-1,528
C. Non-financial services	-850	-862	-877
D. Transfer payments	298	297	475
Long-term capital	1,060	1,709	1,948
E. Public sector	923	1,167	1,168
F. Private sector	137	542	780
Net basic balance	-1,417	-867	-551
G. Short-term capital and errors and omissions	1,935	1,363	1,137
Balance of payments	518	496	586

(1) Includes the financial cost of unpaid services on the public debt.

OVERVIEW OF THE "REINSERTION" PROCESS

The first step in the reinsertion process, completed in September 1991, assured the payment of current maturities due to the multilateral agencies — the IMF and the World Bank — through December 1992.

During this period, Peru did not receive any credit at all from the IMF or the World Bank. Nevertheless, the government continued to apply the stabilization program agreed upon with the IMF and the structural adjustment program agreed upon with the World Bank. As is known, the IMF and the World Bank normally grant loans to countries that implement these programs with the goal, among others, of alleviating the economic and social costs that accompany their application.

In the case of countries with arrears (such as Peru), the IMF and the World Bank argue that they cannot grant loans immediately since these countries must first settle their arrears. This payment of arrears cannot be done through refinancing (such as is common with the Paris Club and the international commercial banks) since this would only worsen the country's image in international capital markets.

The second step in the process of reinsertion was fulfilled in March 1993, when the government paid its arrears with the IMF and the World Bank. In May 1993, the debt with the Paris Club was renegotiated for a period extending through March 1996, the terms of which were discussed above. Similarly, in November 1993, the Peruvian government began negotiations with the international private banks to swap external debt instruments for shares of stock in state firms. This is being done within the framework of the privatization process that is presently under way. Also, the negotiation of a Brady Plan is expected for the second half of 1994.

In a strict sense, the IMF and the World Bank have proceeded to refinance the arrears by creating ad hoc mechanisms (such as the IMF's RAP and the World Bank's "shadow loans"). It should be pointed out, however, that the prolonged period prior to the implementation of these mechanisms meant that during the period of the Reference Program (some two years in the Peruvian case), economic goals continued to be met, but without the receipt of any credit at all. This resulted in such harsh conditions that some have referred to the process as "surgery without anesthesia." This effect was particularly pronounced in Peru, which was experiencing a severe recession (the GDP fell 25 percent from 1988 to 1990), as well as social problems, political violence, drug trafficking, and a cholera epidemic.

From August 1990 through August 1993, the net flow of foreign exchange between Peru and the IMF and the World Bank was negative ($1.371 billion). With the Paris Club, the net flow was positive ($200 million).

Although Peru has managed to resolve its problems in the short term, the long-term payment profile on the external debt (for the years 1994-1999) reveals that it has not been solved. Annual service payments on the external debt for the years 1994-1999 rise to between $2.5 and $3 billion. This cannot be sustained by a country whose annual exports fluctuate around $3 to $3.2 billion.

Diverse analysts maintain that the debt with the Paris Club and the private international banks should be reduced by at least 50 percent. The goal is to be able to handle debt service, above all, because the terms set by the European and North American banks on the Peruvian debt rise to 100 and 70 percent, respectively.[9]

The negotiation of a Brady Plan with the goal of arriving at a comprehensive solution to the commercial bank debt would be framed within the official international strategy of consensus. Consequently, it would not be advantageous for Peru to establish partial mechanisms that are not geared toward an integral solution of the external debt arrears.

The payment of the external debt is equivalent to 20 percent of the Republic's budget in a country in which the tax burden reaches only 10 percent of the GDP. This implies that if external debt payments are to be maintained under the present conditions, then highly restrictive, austere macroeconomic policies that will not permit any reactivation of the economy nor any significant social spending must be implemented.

It is worth noting that during the first two years of the adjustment program, expenditures on social programs were minimal; they did not even represent 0.2 percent of the GDP. In 1993 the government declared that it would satisfy the investment necessary for social support, which is estimated to be 1 percent of the GDP.

As a whole, the reinsertion scheme implied fulfilling the conditions agreed upon with the IMF and the World Bank. There is an explicit gamble that the neoliberal reforms will bring with them structural changes, external financing (in the form of both new investments as well as flows of loan capital), and economic development. Therefore, it is maintained that Peru should follow these policies.

In order to clean up its arrears with the IMF and the World Bank toward the end of the Reference Program in December 1992, Peru signed new agreements with these agencies as a condition for receiving accumulated rights and the "shadow loans."

It can be claimed, therefore, that the ad hoc mechanisms of refinancing arrears with the IMF and the World Bank constitute a new instrument which, on the basis of countries with arrears that need to normalize their relations with the multilateral agencies, permits the continuous application of these policies.

Reinsertion in the international financial system has been one of the top priorities of the Peruvian government. To carry this out, the government itself took the initiative to design a strategy with the multilateral agencies. On many occasions, the Peruvian economic team has gone beyond IMF and World Bank recommendations in applying stabilization and structural adjustment policies. This has meant that, in this case, there has been full agreement between the Peruvian government and the multilateral agencies.

One must consider, however, the hypothesis that the application (whether by this government or another) of economic policies that are not of the same character as those recommended by the IMF and the World Bank might give rise to new problems in Peru's relations with these agencies.

After five years of virtually "broken ties" with the international financial system, the Peruvian government has returned to the path of paying the external debt through the process of reinsertion. As a result of the failure to resolve the long-term debt problem, the negotiations concluded imply debt rescheduling and refinancing with the Paris Club and the international commercial banks. Otherwise, servicing the external debt would become unmanageable, since this would represent 90 percent of annual exports.

The Peruvian government claims that the agreement with the multilateral agencies, the agreement with the Paris Club, and the reinitiation of negotiations with the international commercial banks will be the basis for attracting foreign direct investment, a positive net flow of loans from bilateral and multilateral agencies, and, in the medium run, from international banks.

Simultaneously, the government is confident that this reinsertion into the international financial system, along with the internal application of neoliberal policies, will be a factor that will inspire confidence among Peruvian entrepreneurs, result in new investments, and cause some of the capital that has left the country to return.

NOTES

1. This debt is concentrated among four countries: Brazil, Argentina, Mexico, and Venezuela. The debt with Argentina and Brazil makes up 90 percent of the total.

2. The Support Group was formally constituted June 7, 1991.

3. The program was signed September 11, 1991. Its principal points are the following:

> The government undertook to restore fiscal and monetary discipline during the performance period (July 1991-December 1992). For this period, the balance in the non-financial public sector that had reached annual deficits greater than 5 percent of GDP in 1987-1989 improved to a deficit of 1 percent in 1990 and a surplus of 0.4 percent in 1991. In addition, the quasi-fiscal deficit was limited to 0.5 percent of GDP in 1991 and 0.3 percent in 1992. In agreement with the projected increase in the required monetary offering in order to buy international reserves and service the external debt of the Central Bank, the program assumed an average monthly inflation rate of 5 percent and 1.7 percent for the second half of 1991 and 1992, respectively. An increase in capital inflows of 2 percent of GDP was projected for 1991 and 1992, an increase of the value-added tax to 16 percent (from 14 percent), a simplification of the tariff system, and the beginning of the privatization of public enterprises (letter from Minister Carlos Boloña to Lewis Preston, president of World Bank, February 20, 1992. Published in World Bank, 1992, "Loans to Peru for $300 million").

4. It should be noted that the United States set as a prior condition for forming the Support Group that the Peruvian government sign an agreement on combating drugs. This treaty agreement was signed in May 1991.

5. The country must fulfill four conditions to take advantage of this approach:

> 1) the country must agree to implement a structural adjustment program with the World Bank; 2) the country must embark upon a stabilization plan, if necessary, with the approval and monitoring of the IMF; 3) the country must have a national financial plan. This plan should provide for total liquidation of arrears with the Bank, in the context of an adjustment program in the medium term oriented toward growth....This generally requires strong bilateral support; 4) in this context, the country must continue servicing the Bank's debt that was within the performance period (World Bank 1991c, 1-2).

6. The cut-off date was January 1, 1983, the date when the debt with the Paris Club was rescheduled for the first time.

7. According to the World Bank, these scenarios must be handled cautiously:

The estimates depend on the projection of private capital inflows and the increase in international reserves. It is assumed that during the period 1993 to 1999 there will be annual increases in reserves and positive inflows of private capital, including direct investment related to natural resources and easy access to commercial credits in the short term. We recognize that many of these projections were based on limited information; therefore, we emphasize that this scenario is extremely tentative and ought to be interpreted with much care (World Bank 1992, 25).

8. As it is probable that financial breaches exist, it will be difficult for the Peruvian government to conclude an agreement with the commercial banks (even assuming a "rollover" of 100 percent a year of the aforementioned debt), which requires a significant payment in cash. Nevertheless, they have begun talks that may produce negotiations with private banks and an agreement over part of this debt (World Bank 1992, 25).

9. On this, see *Foro Económico 1992*, 38.

REFERENCES

Banco Central de Reserva. 1993. *Programa Economico Para 1994.* Lima: mimeo.

Campodónico, Humberto. 1991. "Cirugia sin anestesia." *Punto Crítico*(2). Lima, Peru.

Frenkel, Roberto, J.M. Fanelli, and G. Rozenwurcel. 1991. *Crítica al Consenso de Washington.* Lima: CEPES-DESCO-FONDAD, Working Paper.

Government of Peru. 1991a. "Acta acordada de la refinanciación con el Club de París." *El Peruano*, September 30.

Government of Peru. 1991b. "Programa económico del Perú presentado ante el FMI." *El Peruano*, September 30.

Government of Peru. 1993. "Minuta acordada para la consolidación de la deuda del Peru con el Club de Paris." *Boletin del Banco Central de Reserva.*

Hendrick, Oscar, and Javier Pereda. 1993. "Perú: Deuda externa, privatización y estrategia de negociación con la banca comercial." In Banco Central de Reserva, *Gerencia de Estudios Económicos* (Lima), January.

International Monetary Fund. 1991. *Annual Report of the Executive Board for the Financial Year Ended April 30, 1991.* Washington, D.C.: International Monetary Fund.

Latin Finance. 1992. London: Euromoney Publications. May.

Macroconsult. 1991. "Reporte analítico: El acuerdo con el FMI."

Paredes, Carlos. 1993. "El Reto de la deuda peruana con la banca comercial." *Expreso*, November 13.

Ruiz Caro, Ariela, Oscar Ugarteche, and Ministerio de Economia y Finanzas. 1992. "Costos y problemas de la reinserción financiera del Perú." Lima: CEPES-DESCO-FONDAD.

Valdivia-Velarde, Eduardo, Oscar Ugarteche, and Javier Portocarrero. 1992. "Reinserción del Perú con el sistema financiero internacional." *Foro Económico* (4). Lima, Peru.

World Bank. 1991a. "Additional Support for Workout Programs in Countries with Protracted Arrears." Document R91-70. Washington, D.C.

World Bank. 1991b. *The World Bank Annual Report 1991.* Washington, D.C.: The World Bank.

World Bank. 1991c. "Peru: The Bank's Approach to a Country with Protracted Arrears." Document R91-171. Washington, D.C.: The World Bank.

World Bank. 1992. "Report and Recommendation of the President of the IBRD to the Executive Directors on a Proposed Structural Adjustment Loan in an Amount Equivalent to US$300 million to the Republic of Peru." Report No. P-5714 PE. Washington, D.C.: The World Bank.

APPENDIX

Table 1
IMF Loans 1990-1993
(millions of US$)

Rights Accumulation Program	1990	1991	1992	1993	Total
Approved	—	—	—	1,330	1,330
Disbursed	—	—	—	870	870

I. Total loans programmed	1,330
II. Total disbursed	870
III. Total paid by Peru 1990-1993	1,369
IV. Net flow (II-III)	-499

Payments to the IMF

	Depreciation	Interest	Total
1990(*)	57	101	158
1991(*)	46	77	123
1992(*)	47	59	106
1993	18	94	112

Total paid	499
Payment of arrears	870
Total paid 1990-1993	1,369

Sources: Central Reserve Bank and World Bank.

Table 2
World Bank Loans 1990-1993
(millions of US$)

	1990	1991	1992	1993	Total
SAL I loan (shadow)					
Approved	–	–	300	0	300
Disbursed	–	–	0	300	300
SAL II loan (shadow)					
Approved	–	–	300	0	300
Disbursed	–	–	0	300	300
SAL III loan (shadow)					
Approved	–	–	400	0	400
Disbursed	–	–	0	300	300
Privatization loan					
Approved	–	–	–	250	250
Disbursed	–	–	–	75	75
Other (technical assistance)					
Approved	–	–	–	42	42
Disbursed	–	–	–	42	42

I. Total loans programmed	1,292
II. Total disbursed	1,017
III. Total paid by Peru 1990-1993	1,486
IV. Net flow (II-III)	-469

Payments to the IMF (millions of US$)

	Depreciation	Interest	Total
1990(*)	0	0	21
1991(*)	87	115	202
1992	99	98	197
1993	75	91	166

Total paid	586
Payment of arrears	900
Total paid 1990-1993	1,486

Sources: World Bank, Central Reserve Bank.
(*)Central Reserve Bank Annual Reports 1990,1991 and World Bank.

Table 3
IDB Loans 1990-1993
(millions of US$)

	1990	1991	1992	1993	Total
Trade sector					
Approved	0	425	0	0	425
Disbursed	0	375	28	22	425
Financial sector					
Approved	0	0	200	–	200
Disbursed	0	0	100	0	100
Road rehabilitation					
Approved	0	0	210	–	210
Disbursed	0	0	21	0	21
Health sector					
Approved	0	0	0	68	68
Disbursed	0	0	0	0	0
Other (technical assistance, small business)(*)					
Approved	0	44	–	–	44
Disbursed	0	0	8	0	8
Other not disbursed (*)					
Sunat, Foncodes, Ingemmet					
Approved	0	0	9	0	9
Disbursed	0	0	4	0	4

(*) Through July 1993.

I. Total loans programmed	956
II. Total disbursed	558
III. Total paid by Peru 1990-1993	961
IV. Net flow (II-III)	-403

Sources: IDB and Central Reserve Bank.

Table 4
Service of Peru's External Debt 1993-1994
(millions of US$)

	1993	1994
Paris Club	995	964
- Paid	380	347
- Not paid	615	603
Latin America	151	130
- Paid	151	130
- Not paid	0	0
Private banks	411	424
- Paid	10	7
- Not paid	401	417
IFIs	383	435
- Paid	383	435
- Not paid	0	0
Eastern Europe	214	214
- Paid	2	7
- Not paid	212	207
Providers	190	127
- Paid	2	0
- Not paid	188	127
Total	2,344	2,294
- Paid	928	926
- Not paid	1,416	1,354

Note: Balance of payments support loans are excluded.
Source: Peru's Central Bank.

V

THE BOLIVIAN SOLUTION: DEBT REPURCHASE AND DEBT RELIEF

Jaime Delgadillo

THE EXTERNAL DEBT PROBLEM

The external debt is one of the most important problems of Bolivia's political economy. In a country that faces great difficulty in generating sufficient internal savings to confront adequately the challenges of economic growth, external indebtedness and its consequences have represented an obstacle of disproportionate dimensions.

During the past decade, the flow of resources from abroad declined significantly, further aggravating the economic crisis. For a number of years, international financing and assistance were closed to Bolivia. This was true, above all, for loans from the international private banks and the governments of the debt-holding countries. Initial efforts to find a satisfactory, viable solution to this problem were fruitless. Nevertheless, by pursuing a coherent and persistent policy on the external debt, the country succeeded in improving its situation significantly.

EVOLUTION OF BOLIVIA'S EXTERNAL DEBT

Bolivia's external debt, which toward the end of the 1960s was very small, grew substantially from the middle of the 1970s onward.

Table 1 illustrates the evolution of the Bolivian public external debt from 1970 to 1993. In 1985, before the beginning of the debt reduction processes, the country's external debt was comprised of bilateral debt (38 percent), commercial debt with international banks (41 percent), and multilateral debt (21 percent).

As can be seen in the same table, the composition of the Bolivian external debt underwent marked changes over time. A variety of factors

Table 1
Bolivia: Evolution of the Public External Debt, 1970-1993
(millions/billions of US$)

	1970	1975	1980	1985	1986	1987	1988	1989	1990	1991	1992	1993
External debt	480	883	2.182b	3.294b	3.643b	4.289b	4.069b	3.492b	3.779b	3.628b	3.774b	8.830b
Multilateral	26	179	447	872	1.109b	1.289b	1.423b	1.525b	1.705b	1.839b	1.950b	2.077b
Bilateral	246	367	649	1.670b	1.792b	2.260b	2.214b	1.686b	1.806b	1.525b	1.587b	1.669b
Private	208	337	1.086b	752	742	740	432	281	268	264	237	84

Source: Bancó Central de Bolivia.

contributed to this change in the structure of the total amount of external debt. The almost total elimination of the debt with private international banks led to a change in the relative weight of the multilateral and bilateral debt in the total debt. Conversely, obligations with the multilateral agencies increased significantly, thereby increasing these agencies' share of the total debt.

Beginning in 1985 with the subscription of the first draft agreement with the Paris Club, external financing and assistance from bilateral sources again became available to Bolivia. In this manner, the relative importance of the bilateral external public debt also grew within the total. In recent years, successive reductions in the bilateral debt again caused changes in the structure of Bolivia's external obligations. Thus, at present, the most important component is that part corresponding to debt with the multilateral agencies, the principal source of Bolivia's soft and long-term financing.

As of September 30, 1993, data revealed that only 2 percent of Bolivia's total external obligations were with the international private banks. This distinguished Bolivia from other Latin American countries.

Table 1 indicates that the total amount of Bolivia's external public debt rose to $3.83 billion. Of this total, $1.699 billion (48.3 percent) pertains to the bilateral debt, $2.077 billion (54.5 percent) to obligations with multilateral agencies, and only $84 million, as already indicated, to commercial bank debt.

Within the external public debt owed to the multilateral agencies, the principal lender is the Inter-American Development Bank (IDB), which holds some 31 percent. This also makes the IDB Bolivia's principal lender. The International Development Association (IDA) is in second place, with 14.4 percent of the external public debt. Immediately following is the International Bank for Reconstruction and Development (IBRD), which participates with 3.6 percent. The relative participation of each of the remaining multilateral creditors does not reach 6 percent of the total debt.

For bilateral external public debt, Japan appears in first place, with $530 million and some 13.9 percent of the total external obligations. Next comes Germany, whose participation is equal to 9 percent, with $341.7 million. Then follows Belgium ($143.1 million), with 3.8 percent, and the United States ($95.2 million), with 2.5 percent.

As can be seen from Table 1, the most important bilateral lenders are the signatory members of the Paris Club agreements and Brazil. The remaining countries, including other European nations, Eastern European countries, Israel, South Africa, and some Latin American countries, participate with less than 9 percent.

Finally, within the commercial bank debt, the principal financial claims correspond to bonds issued long ago and diverse obligations ($44.4 million). Their participation is equivalent to 1.2 percent of the total external debt. The consortium of banks has a participation of barely 0.3 percent ($9.8 million). The remainder of the debt with private institutions is of no relevance.

ACCOMPLISHMENTS IN RESCHEDULING AND REDUCING THE EXTERNAL DEBT

Since 1985, Bolivia has been implementing a rigorous program of structural adjustment. This program envisages a reordering of Bolivia's international economic and financial relations. In this context, Bolivia has pursued a number of negotiations with bilateral lenders as well as with private international banks.

Bilateral Debt

In order to restructure its external obligations with friendly governments and their financial institutions, Bolivia has resorted to the Paris Club on four occasions. The results were very favorable, as outlined below.

Paris Club I. In 1986, Bolivia went to the Paris Club for the first time, signing a draft agreement on July 25, 1986. On that occasion, twelve countries signed the agreement: the Federal Republic of Germany, Austria, Belgium, Brazil, Denmark, the United States, France, Holland, Israel, Japan, the United Kingdom, and Switzerland.

The amount rescheduled in Paris Club I rose to $510.96 million. New repayment periods were obtained of ten years with a five-year grace period for maturing debt and of ten years with a four-year grace period for overdue obligations. The debt was divided according to tranches: Tranche I referred to debt due as of June 30, 1986, while Tranche II consisted of debt falling due between July 1, 1986, and June 30, 1987. One hundred percent of the amount due on overdue and maturing debts under the heading of capital and interest was rescheduled.

Paris Club II. On November 14, 1988, a new draft agreement with the Paris Club was signed to reschedule Bolivia's bilateral public external debt. This time there were nine signatory countries: the Federal Republic of Germany, Austria, Belgium, the United States, France, Holland, Japan, the United Kingdom, and Switzerland. The amount renegotiated was $247.96 million.

The terms granted to Bolivia were as follow: consolidation and refinancing of 100 percent of the obligations maturing between July 1, 1987, and September 30, 1988, as well as of the debt falling due between October 1, 1988, and December 31, 1989, with a repayment period of eleven years with a seven-year grace period at interest rates to be negotiated directly by Bolivia with each lending country.

Paris Club III. On March 15, 1990, the draft agreement of the Paris Club to reschedule Bolivia's bilateral external debt was negotiated and signed. The amount involved was $262.2 million. This corresponded to current maturities due between January 1, 1990, and December 31, 1991. This rescheduling included regular current maturities in accordance with the original contracts and those previously rescheduled in the drafts of Paris Club I (1986) and of Paris Club II (1988). Ten countries signed this draft agreement: the Federal Republic of Germany, Austria, Belgium, Denmark, the United States, France, Holland, Japan, the United Kingdom, and Switzerland.

Through this arrangement, Bolivia sought to normalize its financial relations with the lending countries, reduce pressures on its balance of payments, and obtain a positive net flow of resources to Bolivia.

On this occasion, the country obtained an exceptional agreement, the Toronto Treatment, which consisted of the following:

- Alternative A: Cancellation of one-third of the total debt to mature during the consolidation period and rescheduling of the remaining two-thirds for a repayment period of fourteen years with an eight-year grace period at interest rates to be negotiated bilaterally on the basis of market conditions.

- Alternative B: A long repayment period applied to concessional debts of twenty-five years with a fourteen-year grace period at interest rates to be negotiated bilaterally on the basis of market conditions.

- Alternative C: Reduction of the interest rates to 3.5 percent per year or 50 percent of the interest rate agreed to bilaterally, rescheduling with a fourteen-year payment and eight-year grace period on obligations maturing during the consolidation period.

The selection of alternatives was as follows:

- Alternative A: France
- Alternative B: Germany, Belgium, the United States, and Holland
- Alternative C: Austria, Denmark, England, and Switzerland
- Alternatives B and C: Japan.

Paris Club IV. On January 24, 1992, the draft agreement of the Paris Club to reschedule Bolivia's bilateral external debt was negotiated and signed for $215.8 million. This corresponded to the obligations maturing between January 1, 1992, and June 30, 1993. This rescheduling included current maturities in accordance with the original contracts and those previously rescheduled in the drafts of Paris Club I (1986), Paris Club II (1988), and Paris Club III (1990). Nine countries signed this agreement: Germany, Austria, Belgium, the United States, France, Holland, Japan, the United Kingdom, and Switzerland.

On this occasion, Bolivia managed to obtain a new exceptional agreement, the Expanded Toronto Treatment, which consisted of the following:

- Alternative A: Cancellation of 50 percent of the principal and interest maturing during the period of consolidation of the amounts not previously renegotiated and of those renegotiated in Paris Club I of 1986 and Paris Club II of 1988 and rescheduling of the remaining 50 percent for a repayment period of twenty-three years with a six-year grace period at interest rates to be negotiated bilaterally on the basis of market conditions.

- Alternative B: Rescheduling of 100 percent of the amount of principal and interest maturing during the consolidation period on debt not previously rescheduled and on the debt renegotiated in Paris Club I and Paris Club II for a twenty-three-year repayment period without a grace period. Interest rates would be reduced in such a manner that the present value of the payment plan would be equivalent to a 50 percent reduction of the amount consolidated.

- Alternative C: Rescheduling of 100 percent of the amount of principal and interest maturing during the consolidation period on debt not previously rescheduled and on the debt renegotiated in Paris Club I and Paris Club II for a twenty-five-year repayment period with a fourteen-year grace period at interest rates to be negotiated bilaterally on the basis of market conditions.

- Official Development Assistance (ODA): The concessional debts would have a long repayment period of twenty-five years with a fourteen-year grace period at interest rates to be negotiated bilaterally and at rates more favorable than the concessional rates.

- Swaps: On a voluntary and bilateral basis, the governments of each lending country may exchange part of their debt for aid to the environment, for development assistance, for equity swaps, or for swaps in the local currency.

The debt rescheduled in Paris Club III will be deferred for a three-year period with biannual payments beginning on July 1, 1993. The selection of alternatives was as follows:

- Alternative A: Germany, France, Holland, and England
- Alternative B: Austria, Belgium, Japan, and Switzerland
- Alternative C: United States.

Participating countries also agreed to hold a meeting in three years' time to consider the problem of the size of Bolivia's debt in order to arrive at a definitive settlement of the problem. The creditors' meeting in the Paris Club would accept an eighteen-month consolidation period only if Bolivia signed an agreement with the International Monetary Fund (IMF) for a fourth year of the Enhanced Structural Adjustment Facility (ESAF) arrangement.

Other Bilateral External Debt Reduction Negotiations. Bolivia also pursued a series of actions aimed at reducing the bilateral debt with countries that were not signatories of the Paris Club. Among these, the following merit highlighting.

- **Argentina**. Argentina was Bolivia's principal bilateral lender. In September 1987, all Bolivia's obligations were rescheduled, resulting in a new payment period of twenty-five years with a fifteen-year grace period at an 8 percent annual interest rate. The amount rescheduled on this occasion was $696.7 million, and the corresponding interest had to be canceled in a similar fashion.

In September 1989, a mutual agreement was reached to cancel the debt of both countries with a cutoff date of July 31, 1989. Bolivia's debit balance to Argentina as of that date reached $850 million. To this figure, unpaid obligations in the amount of $20 million, corresponding to the unpaid balance for the Latin American Integration Association (Asociación Latinoamericana de Integración — ALADI) settlements, must be added.

For its part, Argentina also owed significant amounts to Bolivia in payment for natural gas purchases. Under the heading of overdue invoices for these exports, Argentina's debt rose to $231.5 million. Although there does not exist a clear agreement with this country in regard to the amount, Bolivia estimated that Argentina owed $82 million in interest for arrears on the gas payments; as a result, Argentina's total debt rose to $313.5 million.

In this manner, $850 million of Bolivian debt was canceled against $313.5 million of Argentine obligations.

- **Brazil**. In November 1989, an agreement was reached with Brazil on mechanisms to reduce the Bolivian debt, which consisted of the following alternatives:

  1. Cancellation of overdue obligations through the surrender of Brazilian commercial debt paper acquired by Bolivia on the secondary market. These debt instruments would be exchanged for bilateral Bolivian debt with Brazil to pay off obligations equivalent to their nominal value. By means of this mechanism, over $100 million of Bolivian debt with Brazil already has been reduced in various operations. These operations were realized at 90 and 80 percent of their face value in accordance with a contract agreed to in November 1989.

  2. Creation of a fund in Bolivian currency for a value of 50 percent of the current maturities, through biannual quotas starting June 30, 1990. This fund was aimed at financing a) Bolivian exports to Brazil; b) local contributions for credits from the IDB, the IBRD, and other international agencies, dedicated for investment projects

that Bolivia had classified as priorities; c) cooperation and technical assistance programs from Brazil to Bolivia; and d) Bolivian-Brazilian investments or projects in the area of tourism.

- **Switzerland.** In March 1993, among the European signatories of the Paris Club, Switzerland became the first country to grant unprecedented treatment by canceling a significant portion of Bolivia's debt. On the occasion of bilateral negotiations with Switzerland within the framework of the Paris Club, which were held in La Paz on September 18, 1992, the Bolivian delegation took steps to obtain a cancellation of the debt and to effect swap operations to reduce Bolivian obligations.

The Swiss responded that it was impossible to cancel the debt within the framework of the Paris Club but that it could be done through bilateral efforts. The Swiss delegation explained that Bolivia might benefit from part of the 700 million Swiss francs (SF.) derived from the program "700 Years of the Swiss Confederation," which was designated for the reduction of the external debt of specific countries. This amount was to be used in two ways: SF. 400 million would be used to repurchase bilateral debt contracted on commercial terms, and SF. 300 million, with cofinancing by the World Bank, would be used for environmental projects.

The measures initiated on this occasion led Switzerland to analyze the Bolivian case meticulously. This resulted in the decision to reduce the total bilateral debt, which rose to SF. 52,486,971 ($35.9 million), under the following conditions:

1. Cancellation of 100 percent of the total stock of bilateral debt in its component of foreign currency, which was equivalent to $35.9 million;

2. Conversion of the equivalent of 11 percent of the total amount due into a counterpart fund in local currency for financing environmental, small business, and craft projects;

3. Disbursement of the equivalent of this 11 percent in a single payment to a private bank by April 2, 1993.

This agreement is extremely favorable for Bolivia because 1) it completely eliminates the balance of Bolivia's bilateral external debt with Switzerland, 2) it positively affects Bolivia's balance of payments position by reducing the service on the external debt, and 3) it contributes to social and economic development by creating a counterpart fund of about $4 million designated for financing development and environmental projects.

Switzerland is the first country to grant this treatment, which is unprecedented among the European nations that have signed the Paris Club agreements. It is the first country that grants Bolivia debt forgiveness on debt contracted on commercial terms.

Another part of the agreement reached consisted of eliminating the balance of the total external debt with this country, in that a part (11 percent) is converted into a counterpart fund in local currency for financing environmental, small business, and craft projects. The projects to be financed and the administration of the resources deposited in each fund will be supervised by Swiss Cooperation in Bolivia.

- **Belgium**. In November 1991, Belgium canceled 68 percent of the Bolivian debt in Belgian Francs (BF) corresponding to the consolidation period of Paris Club I. The portion canceled represented BF 447.4 million.

- **Holland**. In the draft agreement of the Paris Club signed in March 1990, Holland selected Alternative B, which consisted of rescheduling the debt for a twenty-five-year payment period with a fourteen-year grace period. In the bilateral negotiations, carried out in October 1990, Bolivia obtained debt forgiveness on one-third of the quotas maturing during the 1990-1991 period; this is equivalent to $7 million and meant that Holland switched from Alternative B to Alternative A of the Toronto Treatment.

By means of the agreement reached with Paris Club IV, Holland conceded to Bolivia Alternative A of the Extended Toronto Treatment, which meant canceling 50 percent of the debt maturing during the consolidation period. This was equivalent to $4.7 million.

- **France**. By means of the agreement reached in Paris Club III, France granted Bolivia Alternative A of the Extended Toronto Treatment, which implied the cancellation of one-third of the debt maturing during the consolidation period. For the lending country, this was equivalent to $8 million.

In Paris Club IV, France adopted Alternative A of the Extended Toronto Treatment, which meant canceling 50 percent of the debt maturing during the consolidation period. This was equivalent to $8 million.

- **Denmark**. In October 1990, negotiations resulted in the cancellation of part of the concessional debt in Danish Kroner (DKr), corresponding to the obligations maturing during the 1991-1994 period. These reached DKr 40.4 million, the equivalent of $7.0 million. A similar request in an amount equivalent to $3 million was accepted for the 1986–1990 period.

- The **United States**. In September 1990, Bolivia, on the basis of President George Bush's Enterprise for the Americas Initiative (EAI), presented the U.S. government with the following proposal:
  1. Reduce Bolivia's bilateral obligations with the United States by 89 percent;

2. Reschedule the remainder of the debt under Alternative B of the terms of the Toronto Treatment, established in the draft signed March 15 in the Paris Club framework;

3. Request that the U.S. government authorize Bolivia to pay interest on the renegotiated remainder, in local currency, to the account of the National Environmental Fund, designated by the EAI as an environmental fund. The interest to be paid to this fund will be used for environmental conservation projects and to sustain development projects implemented by Bolivian governmental and nongovernmental organizations, as well as the entity established by the EAI and the National Environmental Fund, which will be jointly managed by the Bolivian and U.S. governments, with representatives from nongovernmental conservation organizations.

The balance of the debt with the United States was $412.1 million. This broke down into $384.1 million for concessional debts and $28.1 million for commercial debts. Bolivia fulfilled all conditions required to receive the EAI concessions: 1) status as a Latin American country, 2) agreement with the IMF and the World Bank, 3) investment reforms, and 4) efforts to reduce the bilateral and commercial debt. Under EAI, the United States granted Bolivia debt forgiveness on 100 percent of the debt with the U.S. Agency for International Development (AID), which was equivalent to $341.3 million, and on 80 percent of the agricultural debt (P.L. 480), which was equivalent to $30.7 million — in total, some $372 million.

As part of the debt reduction agreement, Bolivia made a commitment to create a $17.2 million fund, to disburse the equivalent of $1 million in local currency twice a year over twenty years, for an environmental fund. Additionally, the agreement involved renegotiating the remaining 20 percent of the P.L. 480 debt ($7.7 million) for a fifteen-year payment period without a grace period at 3 percent annual interest. The interest to be redeemed on this debt ($0.23 million a year) will be deposited in local currency in the environmental fund.

- The **United Kingdom**. On April 14, 1992, through an arrangement with Bolivia, the United Kingdom canceled credits granted by way of the IDB for a value of pounds (£) 3,135,000 ($5.7 million). By means of the agreement reached at Paris Club IV, the United Kingdom also granted Bolivia Alternative A of the Extended Toronto Treatment, which was equivalent to canceling 50 percent of the debt maturing during the consolidation period, which for this lender was equal to $8.6 million.

- **Germany**. In Paris Club IV, Germany granted Bolivia Alternative A of the Extended Toronto Treatment. This was equivalent to cancellation of 50 percent of the debt maturing during the consolidation period; for Germany, this was equivalent to $5.7 million.

- The **Soviet Union**. In 1990, a public external debt renegotiation arrangement was signed between Bolivia and the Vnessheconombank in representation of debt-holding firms in the USSR. This arrangement established that the debt with Soviet entities would be canceled at 11 percent of its nominal value or exchanged for investment bonds at the same present value, with a complete cancellation of interest, recognizing only the part corresponding to the principal. The amount of the debt rose to $9.2 million. As a result of this arrangement, in 1991 measures, the totality of the external debt with the Soviet Union was repurchased in two phases, with 11 percent of its nominal value redeemed.

- **Rumania**. This lender accepted the cancellation of one-third of Bolivia's total debt. According to Bolivian Central Bank figures, this rose to $814,384 in principal and $169,000 in overdue interest, resulting in a total amount of $983,384. The debt forgiveness covered $327,791.

- **Other Countries**. As a result of the Toronto Treatment in Paris Club III and the Extended Toronto Treatment in Paris Club IV, there is a dual benefit since the total stock of the debt has been reduced and there has been a considerable reduction in the volume of payments in current interest.

Commercial Bank Debt

In 1986, Bolivia advised the commercial banks of its inability to effect disbursements to redeem its obligations and launched the idea of repurchasing the debt by using donations for this effect. The secondary market would be the basis for determining the price to be paid for the debt claims. This idea was accepted in principle by the Committee of Banks, which formally requested a proposal to amend the Refinancing Agreement of April 29, 1981. The amendment was presented at the beginning of 1987, and it contained the following basic points:

1. The international banks approved the amendment insofar as they considered Bolivia to be an exceptional country since its economic reality revealed a situation of extreme deterioration, and, therefore, it was considered an International Development Association (IDA) country by the World Bank. At the same time, they recognized that the Bolivian government was adopting very harsh, yet adequate, measures to improve the economic situation.

2. The Bolivian government would use donations to repurchase the debt only during a four-month period. During this four-month period, the "Pari-Passu" clauses included in the 1981 agreement would not be of obligatory compliance. On the other hand, each of the banks would receive in payment an identical percentage for each dollar of capital lent.

3. The Bolivian debt could be exchanged for "qualified investments."

In January 1988, the Offer Memorandum was presented. Bolivia offered a price of eleven cents per dollar of capital lent. In addition, the memorandum included an offer to the debt-holding banks to exchange external debt for investment bonds issued by the Bolivian Central Bank, with a present value at the moment of issuance of the bond equivalent to 11 percent of the capital owed and a twenty-five-year maturation, at which time the bonds would reach 100 percent of their face value. This program also envisaged a complete cancellation of all types of interest.

The aim of exchanging the external debt for Bolivian investment bonds was twofold. On the one hand, the government sought to withdraw external debt and, on the other, to attract investments to the country.

On April 2, 1993, a new agreement was signed with the private international banks. It involved the following mechanisms: 1) repurchase in cash of the commercial debt for sixteen cents on every dollar of principal owed, 2) issuance of thirty-year exchange bonds to be swapped for commercial debt, and 3) issuance of short-term (nine-month) social/environmental bonds to be exchanged for Bolivian commercial debt titles.

These options constituted total payment and consequently the redemption of the original debt, including overdue past interest and any other payments arising from the debt or its service, with the lender's express renunciation of all rights or action related to it.

In the overall process of reducing the commercial debt, the following amount was reduced:

By the buy-back:	$253.1 million	(29.6%)
By donations:	$15.9 million	(2.3%)
By bond swaps:	$230.1 million	(41.6%)
By operation 1993:	$170.0 million	(25.0%)
Total Reduction:	$669.1 million	(98.5%)

In accordance with the process described above, since the repurchase operations and the bilateral negotiations with the Paris Club began, Bolivia managed to reduce $2.403 billion, the equivalent of 56 percent of the total debt as of the end of 1987 ($4.289 billion).

This reduction, which in some cases includes capital and interest, breaks down in the following manner (figures in millions of dollars):

International Private Banks:	$669.1
Argentina:	$870.0
United States:	$373.0
Brazil:	$373.0
Paris Club IV:	$67.0
Paris Club III:	$15.0
Switzerland:	$35.9
Belgium (BF 657):	$19.5
Soviet Union:	$9.2
Denmark (DKr 40.8 + $1.8):	$7.8
United Kingdom:	$5.7
Austria:	$1.0
Rumania:	$0.3
Total:	$2,402.5

EXTERNAL DEBT POLICIES

In the face of somber prospects, particularly during the first years of the 1980s, it was necessary for Bolivia to have at hand a clear, well-defined external debt policy and, at the same time, a strategy intended to achieve a series of objectives in this area.

Commercial Debt Policy

In the case of the commercial debt, which presently amounts to 2 percent of the balance of the debt after the repurchase operations that were effected, it is only necessary to continue the economic reforms initiated in 1985 to attain a progressive reopening of commercial financing.

Bilateral Debt Policy

From the structure of the Bolivian public external debt, it follows that the emphasis of national efforts to reduce the stock of the debt must center on the bilateral debt. Bolivia rescheduled part of these obligations in the framework of the Paris Club in 1986, 1988, 1990, and 1992 and obtained generous repayment and grace periods as well as favorable financial conditions. In the March 15, 1990, meeting, Bolivia obtained the Toronto Treatment, which until then had been reserved solely for the Southern Saharan countries. Furthermore, in January 1992, Bolivia managed to obtain the so-called "Trinidad Package," becoming only the fourth country in the world to have obtained this exceptional treatment.[1]

Multilateral Debt Policy

In regard to the multilateral debt, it is presently impossible to proceed with its refinancing or rescheduling unless the constitutive arrangements of the principal creditors, the IDB and the World Bank, are modified. Modification would require approval by the member countries with the greatest number of quotas — that is, the group of ten most industrialized countries — which does not appear to be probable. Therefore, service on the debt with these agencies must be realized in the normal manner, especially since the net flow of resources with these institutions is positive for Bolivia.

Policy on External Indebtedness

For many years, Bolivia lacked a clear policy on external indebtedness. Two basic reasons caused this omission: 1) the nearly unlimited supply of external resources, which made it very easy to obtain financing from the international private banks and 2) the exuberant management that successive de facto governments made of international financing. This situation resulted in the implementation of many unprofitable, overblown, or unproductive projects. It is for this reason that, beginning in 1985, Bolivia began to define a clear policy regarding external indebtedness based on the following aspects:

1. Financing should be obtained fundamentally from the multilateral agencies (IBRD, IDB, IMF, the Andean Development Corporation [Corporación Andina de Fomento, CAF], [Fundo Andino de Reserva, FAR], and so on) on soft terms with long repayment periods to finance projects that generate employment, internal value-added, and additional exports.

2. The public sector should avoid contracting short-term commercial credits and credits at high interest rates.

3. Contracting external credits for the public sector presently requires prior government approval. The organs responsible for defining all aspects of external debt policy had existed in transitory form as the Special Committee for External Debt (Comité Especial para la Deuda Externa, CEDEX). By means of Supreme Decree No. 21501, the Commission on the External Debt (Comisión de la Deuda Externa) was instituted in 1987.

Later, the Committee on External Financing (Comité de Financiamiento Externo, COFINEX) was formed in January 1990. It is made up of the Ministers of Planning, Foreign Relations, and Finance, the President of the Central Bank of Bolivia, and an Executive Secretary. This agency is in charge of defining all aspects of external debt policy: the contracting of new financing, debt negotiation and reduction, the definition of mechanisms for attracting and mobilizing external resources, and so forth.

External Debt Control and Tracking Policy

The institutional changes that occurred in Bolivia following the promulgation of Supreme Decree No. 21060 in 1985 resulted in the Central Bank's loss of efficiency in controlling and tracking the external debt. At a certain point, the technical, operational, and statistical management of the external debt became an important stumbling block for the development of negotiations, fulfillment of accords, and control of the external debt. Even though these deficiencies have largely been overcome, in 1990 it was necessary to define a very clear policy in this regard. This was expressed in the following points:

1. Strengthening and supplying of the Central Bank of Bolivia with the means that would permit the issuing entity efficiently to fulfill its functions, in particular, those regarding the external debt. This involved giving back to the bank its role as the monetary and financial authority and concentrating in it the different tasks regarding the debt that had been dispersed in different agencies: the Ministry of Foreign Affairs, the Ministries of Planning and Coordination, Finances, and Hydrocarbons.

2. Establishment of a system to monitor, register, control, and track the public external debt that covers the whole public sector.

3. Creation of the Committee of External Financing.

Policy of Reordering the Debt

In concordance with the previous points, other important steps are needed to reorder the external debt:

1. Continued negotiations on the bilateral debt within the framework of the Paris Club with the goal of obtaining permanent relief of this debt;

2. Negotiations in highly concessional terms with the socialist countries and other lenders on the external debt;

3. Adherence to the financial arrangements previously subscribed by Bolivia, attaining improvements through negotiations;

4. Seeking, through these negotiations, the concession of a positive net flow of resources to the country, that is, inflows that exceed the service on the debt.

The Role of the External Debt in the Adjustment Program

In the Bolivian case, the problem of the external debt followed the trajectory of the crisis of indebtedness undergone by the majority of Latin American countries: After receiving large flows of capital which stimulated growth during the 1970s, the debt was transformed into an obstacle for development in the 1980s, once the stream of net transfers of credit reverted.

Clearly, Bolivia registered positive net transfers of medium- and long-term credit during all operations carried out from the 1970s until 1981. Nevertheless, between 1982 and 1985, during the period of most severe crisis for the Bolivian economy, the country had to remit net flows abroad which rose to over 5 percent of the gross domestic product (GDP) during some years of this period. This situation — combined with significant capital flight, declines in international prices for exports, and certain errors of economic management — led to a systematic fall in production and a sharp increase in internal prices which led to a hyperinflationary process that reached its peak in 1985.

It should be noted that during this period — more accurately, between 1980 and 1983 — Bolivia resorted to rescheduling the principal of the debt with the private international banks on commercial terms. This situation, which at the time was framed within the dominant international strategy of debt management, basically consisted of viewing the debt problem as nothing more than a problem of a lack of liquidity, which is why the indebted countries had to resort to economic adjustment. This strategy was unsuccessful and instead provoked depressive effects and created conditions of greater risk that debt service payments would not be fulfilled.

It should be remembered that as of December 31, 1985, the balance of the Bolivian debt in arrears rose to over $1 billion, the equivalent of almost one-fourth of the GDP. This led to costs to the country that resulted from a unilateral restriction of payments.

When the economic adjustment program was implemented in August 1985, a new approach was also taken on the external debt strategy. This consisted of reducing the burden of the debt. In 1987, after the failure of the original Baker Plan, the international debt strategy recognized the existence of high levels of overindebtedness and the need to reduce them. In this context, Bolivia was one of the leading countries in reducing an important amount of its debt with the international private banks. Thus, between 1988 and 1989, the government, using resources donated by the international community, repurchased almost two-thirds of its debt with the commercial banks, paying a price of eleven cents per dollar. This situation, combined with the renegotiation of the bilateral debt in Paris Club I, II, III, and IV as well as the increased financial support granted by the multilateral agencies, permitted a return to positive flows of resources in the 1986-1993 period.

The operation of repurchasing the debt with private international banks led to a reduction in the weight of this type of debt in Bolivia's overall balance from 36 percent in 1980 to 2 percent in 1993.

The successful negotiations to reduce the bilateral debt translated into a decrease in the share of this debt in the overall debt, as well as in a sharp reduction in its incidence in the payment of debt services. In regard to the multilateral debt, which as of March 1992 represented almost 50 percent of the total, a policy should be followed that, basically, will perpetuate positive transfers of credits from these institutions to Bolivia.

The Bolivian strategy for fixing the debt problem has demonstrated that, in practice, it is possible to pursue many steps — some traditional, others that are new and imaginative — with the fundamental goal of reducing the burden of the debt and thereby dedicating greater resources to growth and, in the final analysis, development. After realizing a profound economic adjustment from 1985 onward, Bolivia, with the support of the international financial community, has successfully acted to solve the problem of the debt. This action, combined with the fact that every country presents particular characteristics with regard to its economy and, principally, to the structure and composition of its debt, demonstrates that the international strategy of managing the debt should involve case by case negotiations.

STRATEGIES TOWARD THE FUTURE

The problem of external indebtedness has placed serious limitations on the resumption of economic development. The crisis of external indebtedness of the early 1980s has had dramatic repercussions upon the economies of all the developing countries, particularly those of Latin America and the Caribbean as well as the African countries. Onerous debt service payments, despite the progress that has been made in debt reduction, constitute a drain on valuable resources that could be dedicated to financing highly productive, labor-intensive projects that generate value-added, which would contribute to mitigating the unfavorable social effects of the economic crisis.

Levels of investment have fallen at an alarming rate during the past decade; this decline, when combined with the scarcity of internal savings in the majority of the countries of the region, as a logical consequence has prevented a growth in production. Additionally, the flows of external financing have declined, aggravating the structural disequilibria of these countries. In this manner, real wages have suffered a pronounced deterioration, per capita income has fallen, and internal prices have risen, in many cases, by uncontrollable proportions.

The efforts made by governments to put their economies on a sound footing have almost always run up against the heavy burden of servicing the debt. The efforts to increase and diversify exports, substitute imports, modernize the productive apparatus, maintain fiscal balance, and normalize relations with external lenders are all hindered by the debt service.

Despite the progress observed over the past several years in the treatment of the less-developed countries' debt, the underlying problem has not been solved; this is a point that Bolivia has raised repeatedly and in a number of international forums. As yet, not all possible actions to find real solutions have been exhausted, nor does there appear to be sufficient awareness among external creditors that the problem must be faced in a context of shared responsibility among debtors and lenders.

The severe adjustment programs that have been carried out, principally by the Latin American countries, have not had any counterpart from the external debt holders. While the less-developed nations have sought to eliminate their balance of payments deficits and to liberalize their international trade, the developed countries have exercised drastic tariff restrictions and excessive protectionism; they have severely reduced financing for the debtor nations and maintained enormous fiscal deficits.

This leads to another crucial point in the solution of the debt problem. A positive net flow of resources is required by the countries of the region. It cannot be expected that a country 1) that generates a low level of internal savings, 2) whose access to international markets is limited by protectionism in the developed countries, 3) that increasingly receives fewer financial resources from these same countries, and 4) that executes harsh processes of structural adjustment with high social costs should also be obligated to observe rigid norms regarding the fulfillment of its external obligations. It is necessary, therefore, to find adequate and effective paths to a true solution to the external debt affliction.

It is necessary to distinguish the different forms that the external indebtedness problem assumes in the different countries. Each nation has its own particularities that must be analyzed. Generalizations can be pernicious. In this sense, an individual treatment is indispensable not only for each type of debt but for each country. The structure of the external debt is different in each case; therefore, different solutions should be sought, though all are aimed at the same end: the reduction of the stock of the debt.

Alternatives for Reducing the Stock of the Debt

Based on analysis of the Bolivian experience, in this section are presented a number of alternatives aimed at reducing the stock of the external debt.

Commercial Debt

The bases for reducing the existing debt with international private banks are outlined by the Brady Plan. Bolivia concurs with the proposal that the solution of the commercial debt be framed within the reduction of this debt, as measured by values on the secondary market. Even though some countries are prevented from cancelling the totality of their debts by directly purchasing their respective titles on the secondary market because different clauses obstruct this repurchase as does the lack of resources, it is nonetheless possible to implement various mechanisms to reduce the debt.

One difficulty must be carefully analyzed, however. Due to the configuration of the debt owed by the majority of the Latin American and Caribbean countries, a direct repurchase of the commercial debt would entail a reduction in the flow of fresh capital from private international banks to the region, which might have serious consequences for those economies that require an important flow of resources from these financial agencies.

With the opening observed in the countries of the socialist orbit to the capital markets, the private international banks may deem it more advantageous to grant loans to these countries rather than the countries of the region. The proposal to reduce the debt with these organizations through the utilization of the secondary market may accelerate such a decision, with the consequent substantial reduction of new disbursements.

Official Debt with Creditor Governments

The Bolivian experience in regard to official debt with creditor nations indicates that the present mechanisms employed by the Paris Club are insufficient for a substantial solution of this debt.

Even though the continued renegotiations represent short-term relief for the balance of payments, they do no more than postpone the solution, creating at the same time a snowball effect since the total volume of the debt continues to increase for the future. As a result, the use of more flexible, effective, and imaginative mechanisms becomes imperative.

After having gone for the fourth time to the Paris Club, Bolivia has received the Trinidad Package, which constitutes a first step in the solution of its debt problem. Nevertheless, on this basis, it is possible to imagine new elements that would permit a more enduring solution to the debt of the less-developed countries of the region. For this reason, we propose:

1. Cancellation of part of the stock of the bilateral debt. The percentage to be canceled could depend upon the socioeconomic conditions prevailing in each country.

2. Reduction of interest rates. The Trinidad Treatment envisages the reduction of interest rates. This reduction should be even greater.

3. Incorporation of already rescheduled debts. In future negotiations, already rescheduled debts could be incorporated under the terms of Trinidad.

4. Cutoff date. The inclusion of certain debts contracted after the cutoff date would permit additional relief in some cases — to be negotiated with each country in particular — as long as this does not preclude the inflow of new financial resources.

5. Elimination of the De Minimis clause. In this manner, small debts (in some cases) would be included in future restructurings.

6. Option of repayment in local currencies to finance social projects. Funds in local currencies of the debtor countries could be formed, with the purpose of using debt service payments to finance projects that are noninflationary and that generate employment.

7. Conversion of development assistance debts into donations. Concessional obligations could be converted into donations, thereby reducing the stock of the debt.

8. Repayment of official obligations with bonds or securities of the debtor states. This mechanism permits a substantial saving of resources which, under these conditions, could be dedicated to internal investment.

9. Exchange of the nominal value of the bilateral debt for titles of other countries' commercial debt. The acquisition of titles of the commercial external debt of the creditor countries on the international market would permit the debtor states to pay all their obligations with these countries using lower amounts than those required for traditional payment since the real value of these titles is lower than their face value in this market.

Debt with Multilateral Agencies

The principal obstacle for renegotiating obligations with the multilateral agencies lies in the constituent arrangements of institutions such as the World Bank and the IDB. An eventual modification of these arrangements does not appear to be at hand, nor is one probable in the near future. What is possible is to ensure that these agencies provide sufficient, timely, fresh resources that allow the member countries to confront tasks of economic development with determination.

Bureaucratic obstacles and the rigid norms for the utilization of resources only obstruct the efforts of governments to improve their inhabitants' living conditions. Greater flexibility in the amount of loans and timing of loan approvals is indispensable. These should fundamentally take into account the quality of the countries' policies of structural change, as well as the programs and projects presented, and not simply mathematical criteria regarding the distribution of resources.

A positive net flow of resources to the countries of the region, a reduction of interest rates and commitment fees, and an extension of the repayment periods should,therefore, be sought with the aim of reducing the transfer of resources abroad.

Intraregional Debt

Intraregional debt constitutes an important part of many countries' total debt; therefore, it is imperative that effective solutions be sought for this problem. The conditions requested by the debtor countries of the region to their creditors from outside the region should also be reflected in the treatment given to the debtor nations of Latin America and the Caribbean. In this very same manner, the proposals made regarding the bilateral debt could be wholly applied in this case, above all with regard to canceling a portion of the obligations and to exchanging all the nominal value of the bilateral debt for commercial debt titles of the creditor, acquired by the debtor at their market value.

At the same time, the creditor countries of the region should begin to apply the mechanisms designed in their attempts to convert the Río Club into an effective forum for solving the problem of the intraregional debt. Among the basic principles behind the creation of this organization was granting favorable terms and conditions to the relatively less-developed debtor countries. Similarly, a number of the mechanisms previously pointed out were envisaged, such as the reduction of the stock of the debt, debt title swaps, the transformation of the debt into investments and its conversion into debt in the local currency. Regarding debt service, a number of possibilities were mentioned: the total or partial payment with external debt titles of the creditor country (no impediments prevent this from being done with the principal), the concession of longer payment periods, payments in kind, and the cancellation in local currency. The creditor countries should begin by setting an example through the utilization of these mechanisms as a sign of good will toward an effective solution of the intraregional external debt problem.

CONCLUSIONS AND RECOMMENDATIONS

B olivia has advanced a long way toward the solution of its severe external debt problems. The experience of the past years provides clear evidence that the appropriate combination of macroeconomic policies directed at maintaining stability and promoting growth, the adoption of important structural adjustment measures designed to institute a market economy, limiting the role of the state to activities of a social order, along with adequate policies to renegotiate and contract external debt have produced satisfactory results along the difficult road to restoring the long-term viability of the economy. The adoption of a national external debt policy, which has been implemented by different governments, has achieved a reduction in a significant part of the Bolivian external debt.

The Bolivian case is illustrative of the experience of a highly indebted, low-income country which has managed to convert a situation of insolvency and almost no international credibility into one of visible reduction both of the stock of the debt and of the service. The country has thereby restored creditor confidence and credibility. The facts fundamentally translate into net positive flows with Bolivia's principal creditors during the past years.

In the international context, Bolivia possesses the best record of debt reduction in its group. It is also one of the few countries to have made progress simultaneously in solving various types of debt, particularly the commercial and bilateral debts, both within and outside of the Paris Club.

The process of negotiating the Bolivian debt over the course of the last seven years has resulted in a substantial modification in the size and structure of the debt. Presently, the country's having virtually eliminated the commercial debt, the bulk of the debt is concentrated among the multilateral financing agencies and bilateral creditors which are members of the Paris Club. The service on the external debt, still equivalent to an important level of exports, has been reduced significantly and is dedicated primarily to covering obligations with the international financial agencies such as the World Bank, the IDB, the World Bank group, the IMF, and CAF.

Maintaining an arrangement with the IMF allows Bolivia to negotiate its debts with the Paris Club and to opt for new financing from the World Bank and the IDB as well as from the countries affiliated to the Club, such as the United States, Japan, Germany, Belgium, France, Italy, Spain, England, Switzerland, Holland, and others.

The insufficient level of internal savings in Bolivia prevents the country from financing an adequate level of economic activity and consequently forces Bolivia to resort to external financing in order to achieve an acceptable rhythm of growth. Nevertheless, the country must persist with the policy of contracting new debt under appropriate conditions, at long terms and with low rates of interest, in order to avoid a new debt problem in the future. Likewise, the majority of the new debts for the public sector should be channeled toward activities of a social order and investments in basic infrastructure, leaving the financing of productive activities to private investment.

Given the present levels of the stock and service of the debt and the growth of multilateral debt, Bolivia needs to procure a new and substantial reduction of its bilateral debt within the framework of the Paris Club. This reduction, if it is achieved at the appropriate time and to a significant magnitude, would contribute substantially to consolidating confidence in macroeconomic stability, to attracting greater flows of private investment, and to improving levels of internal savings. The reduction of the debt should be accompanied by imaginative programs of conversion or exchange of the remainder of the debt, for diverse social programs, such as healthcare, education, rural development, alternative development, and environmental protection, insofar as the monetary and fiscal initiatives permit.

Bolivia's future progress with respect to the external debt will most certainly rest upon the quality and timeliness of the country's macroeconomic management.

NOTE

1. Prior to Bolivia, only Benin, Tanzania, and Nicaragua had obtained the "Trinidad Package."

REFERENCES

Banco Central de Bolivia. 1985-1992. Annual Reports.

Comite de Financiamiento Externo, several documents.

Delgadillo, Jaime. 1992. "La Crisis de la Deuda Externa y sus Soluciones: La Experiencia de Bolivia," Banco Central de Bolivia, La Paz, November.

Government of Bolivia. Memorandum on Economic Policies, presented to the Paris Club meetings.

VI

Mexico's Strategy for Reducing Financial Transfers Abroad

José Angel Gurría and Sergio Fadl

Introduction

In 1989, the process of restructuring Mexico's foreign debt, which began in 1982, entered its fifth stage. This stage, which ended on February 4, 1990, with the signing of an agreement between the Mexican government and the lending banks, differed fundamentally from the four preceding stages:

1. Its basic goal was to halt the net transfer of resources abroad and permanently solve the problem of foreign debt overhang by reducing the outstanding debt and its service; earlier negotiations sought relief, basically, by means of rescheduling principal payments and by contracting new credit.

2. It occurred after seven consecutive years of high inflation and economic stagnation that had led to a severe deterioration in the population's levels of welfare; therefore, as rapidly as possible, it was necessary to arrive at an agreement favorable to Mexico whose central objective would be economic growth with price stability.

3. The amounts involved were so large that during the negotiations, it was necessary to request that the governments of the lending countries grant their support by changing a number of regulations to allow the banks to absorb possible losses.

4. It established a precedent of great importance for agreements between creditors and highly indebted developing countries; for the first time, foreign debt overhang was recognized as an obstacle for the economic growth of these countries. This required an immediate reduction of net transfers of resources to a level compatible with economic development.

5. The negotiations were guided by recognition of the coresponsibility among debtors and creditors. Thus, from the outset, reductions in the principal and interest rates were sought from the lending banks.

To present a broad view of Mexico's most recent foreign debt negotiation and its effect on the national economy, it is helpful first to consider the recent background to the problem of debt overhang and foreign debt policy during the period 1982-1988, as well as the macroeconomic context preceding the last renegotiation. The present paper first reviews the macroeconomic context during the period 1979-1982 and the origins of Mexico's debt overhang. Second, it analyzes the restructuring of the foreign debt between 1982 and 1988, as well as its implications for the macroeconomic framework. In the third section, the effects of the foreign debt on the economy are analyzed. The fourth section examines the specific objectives of the foreign debt policy after 1989, the strategy followed by Mexico throughout the negotiations with its international creditors, and the agreements that were reached. The most recent programs and actions in debt administration are analyzed in the fifth section. The final section presents conclusions.

ORIGINS OF MEXICO'S DEBT OVERHANG, 1979-1982

The foreign debt policies pursued between 1979 and 1981 were based on the then-fundamental strategic objective of promoting economic growth and employment. To achieve these goals, public spending grew rapidly; this growth in expenditures was out of proportion with the dynamics of public sector income, despite the rise of oil exports to extraordinarily high levels during these years. Thus, while the public sector deficit on average represented 6.7 percent of the gross domestic product (GDP) during 1977-1978, in the following biennium, it rose to 7.6 percent and reached 14.1 percent in 1981.[1]

In large measure, the expansion of the public deficit was financed with foreign loans. During this period, contracting resources abroad was profitable in light of the prevailing interest rates and the favorable outlook for oil income — large deposits of oil had been discovered, and oil prices were expected to rise significantly over the medium term. At the same time, private investment, stimulated by the expansion of the economy, offered high rates of return; as a result, many projects were also financed with foreign resources. Furthermore, the liquidity of the international financial markets made it possible to contract resources with a minimum of requisites. By the end of 1981, the total foreign debt was $74.861 billion, of which $52.961 billion was the public sector's. From 1977 to 1981, the foreign debt increased $33.361 billion.

The dynamism of aggregate demand and the maintenance of the exchange rate resulted in an accelerated appreciation of the real exchange rate to far above historical levels. Despite the income from oil exports between 1977 and 1982, the cumulative current account balance of payments deficit was $33.382 billion. The items that most contributed to this deficit were the non-oil trade balance (with a total deficit of $51.629 billion) and the financial services balance (negative $32.624 billion). Items showing a surplus were the oil trade balance (with a cumulative balance of $44.115 billion) and tourism ($5.019 billion).

It is clear that the evolution of the economy was basically dependent on oil exports. Similarly, with the growth in the outstanding foreign debt, service payments came to represent a considerable burden, such that the debt also became a source of vulnerability for the economy. Thus, the economy's performance depended primarily on two variables that were beyond the control of economic policy: international interest rates and international oil prices.

Beginning in the second half of 1981, the fall in oil prices provoked a sharp deterioration in the current account of the balance of payments. Total oil exports rose by only 40 percent, whereas between 1977 and 1980, they had grown on average by over 100 percent per year. On the other hand, the dynamism of non-oil exports fell drastically. This was due to 1) the fall in international prices of some of Mexico's export products (primarily raw materials); 2) the smaller surplus available for export, due to the expansion of internal demand; and 3) an increasingly overvalued peso, the result of maintaining a fixed exchange rate between 1978 and 1981 in the midst of an inflationary context (the real exchange rate appreciated about 30 percent during this period). Furthermore, given the increase in the external debt during these years, total interest payments abroad rose from 2.2 percent of the GDP in 1977 to 3.8 percent in 1981.[2] This led Mexico to resort to the commercial banks to obtain a greater flow of short-term financing.

The events of 1981 gave rise to the formation of unfavorable expectations regarding the economy's evolution. This can be seen in the magnitude of capital flight during 1981 which was estimated at $11.648 billion (Gurría 1988). Capital flight explains why the net foreign indebtedness for this year far surpassed the need for external resources determined by the current account deficit.

By 1982, the economic environment had become extremely unfavorable, and a number of changes in economic policy took place. In general, these changes only further aggravated the climate of uncertainty regarding prospects for economic recovery. The imbalance in public finances, the deterioration in the current account of the balance of payments, and the overvaluation of the exchange rate continued to spur capital flight, which for 1982 was estimated at $6.490 billion. Faced with this situation and the shortage of additional foreign loans, due to the risk involved for the lending banks, Mexico found itself unable to fulfill its obligations with the international financial community on the originally agreed terms.

THE RESTRUCTURING OF THE FOREIGN DEBT, 1982-1988

This section reviews foreign debt policies and the results of the three restructurings effected during the 1982-1988 period, as well as the search for and implementation of complementary means of reducing the outstanding foreign debt.

First Restructuring, 1982-1983

Due to the severe shortage of foreign exchange, on August 22, 1982, Mexico requested from the commercial banks a three-month deferral on payments of the principal of the public foreign debt, which amounted to $8.144 billion.[3] Meanwhile, negotiations were begun with the International Monetary Fund (IMF), the governments of the lending countries, and the commercial banks themselves to contract fresh resources. In December 1982, Mexico requested that the commercial banks restructure $23.150 billion of current maturities of principal, due between August 23, 1982, and December 31, 1984. The negotiations extended through August 1983. Between August and October 1983, contracts were subscribed to restructure the debt of the federal government and all other public sector entities. This debt was rescheduled for an eight-year period with a four-year grace period, with a spread of 1 7/8 percentage points over the London Interbank Offered Rate (LIBOR) and of 1 3/4 percentage points over the prime rate. This resulted in significant relief for the balance of payments and simultaneously provided the incoming government with greater time to implement its economic program.

To finance its 1983 economic program, Mexico requested $5 and $2 billion in new credits from the commercial banks and the Paris Club, respectively. The loan from the commercial banks was contracted with a six-year repayment period with a three-year grace period, at interest rates of LIBOR plus 2 1/4 points and of the prime rate plus 2 1/8 points. These high surcharges reflected the greater risk faced by the lending banks and the lack of understanding of the phenomenon being faced.

As for the private sector foreign debt, by December 1982, its outstanding balance was over $23 billion. Of this debt, two-thirds had been contracted with the commercial banks with maturities of two years or less; the remaining one-third consisted of short-term credits. It was necessary to restructure the corresponding payments, since the 1982 devaluations made the liabilities of many indebted firms practically unpayable.[4]

First was expressed the need to ameliorate the private sector's debt amortizations profile and, second, indebted Mexican firms needed to receive loans in dollars without running exchange risks. To handle the payments of the private debtors properly, the *Fideicomiso para la Cobertura de Riesgos Cambiarios, Ficorca* (Trust Fund to Cover Exchange Risks) was created in March 1983. This trust fund operated according to the principles of international foreign exchange futures markets and functioned to minimize the exchange risk of private firms holding debits in foreign currencies and payable outside of the country, contracted prior to December 20, 1982. In October 1983, the foreign private debt with the commercial banks was restructured in the amount of $12 billion with an eight-year repayment and a four-year grace period.

Second Restructuring, 1984-1985

The 1982-1983 restructuring was concerned primarily with restructuring part of the principal and obtaining new financing. Nevertheless, there remained in force a repayment schedule on the principal — subsequent to December 31, 1984 — incompatible with Mexico's real capacity for payment. The Mexican government wanted a broader solution on a multiyear basis. As a result, negotiating efforts centered on three aspects: 1) to restructure the payments on the principal maturing between 1985 and 1990, 2) to improve the terms agreed to in 1982 and 1983, and 3) to obtain new loans for the 1984 economic program. As to this last point, in April 1984, a loan for $3.8 billion was subscribed with 500 commercial banks in order to satisfy foreign exchange requirements for that year. This loan was negotiated on better terms than those agreed to in March 1983.[5]

In 1985, the restructuring of approximately $48 billion was effected. This amount consisted of about $20 billion maturing between 1985 and 1990, the slightly more than $23 billion that had been restructured in 1983, and the $5 billion in new loans obtained during the same year. The total of $43 billion (the sum of the first components) was negotiated for a fourteen-year term, with a five-year grace period, and a program of increasing payments starting in 1986. Of the remaining $5 billion, $1.2 billion would be paid in 1985, and the rest would be liquidated over a ten-year period with a five-year grace period. Regarding interest rates, it was agreed to eliminate the prime rate as the rate of reference and to substitute the LIBOR. Mexico also obtained a considerable reduction in the surcharges: The spread applied to the $43 billion would be 7/8 percent during the first two years, 1 1/8 percent during the following five years, and 1 1/4 percent during the last seven years. Furthermore, the margins applicable to the $5 billion in new money from 1983 were adjusted to 1 1/2 points over the LIBOR and 1 1/8 points over the rate that replaced the prime rate.

Despite the progress made between 1982 and 1985 in terms of deferrals on the principal and the reduction in surcharges, the magnitude of interest payments and the scarcity of fresh external resources resulted in an average annual net transfer of resources abroad of 6.8 percent of the GDP over these four years.[6] The fact that Mexico went from being a net recipient to a net exporter of capital exerted strong pressures of recession upon the economy

— on average, in real terms, the GDP grew only 0.4 percent — and the principal indicators of the foreign debt burden showed no signs of significant improvement.[7]

It was evident that interest payments continued to restrict the availability of resources. This situation was aggravated by the rise in international interest rates, the fall in export revenues — due to the deterioration in the terms of trade during this period — and the practically nonexistent flow of new loans. As a result, the Mexican government began to advocate an *adjustment with growth*, since this was the only way that the country could recover its capacity to pay, and growth required fresh resources. This new approach meshed with the Baker Plan, proposed in October 1985 by the then-U.S. Secretary of the Treasury, James Baker. The plan suggested that the commercial banks grant a total of $20 billion over three years in new loans to the debtor nations, with the goal of promoting global programs that sustain economic growth. These resources, which represented barely 25 percent of the interest payments of the fifteen debtor countries included in the plan, were to be complemented by resources from the multilateral agencies and each country's trade surplus. It was a "cash flow" concept, but it contained no solid proposal for generating growth, since it assumed negative net transfers as a structural component of the plan.

Third Restructuring, 1986-1987: The Search for Alternative Solutions

In 1986, the price of Mexican export oil fell 50.4 percent in relation to the 1985 average price. This implied a loss of approximately $8 billion in revenue, some 6 percent of the GDP. To this must be added the economic losses that accompanied the two earthquakes in September 1985, which according to some estimates rose to 2 percent of the 1985 GDP. Foreseeing a possible inability to service the foreign debt, Mexico initiated new contacts with the international financial community.

In June 1986, Mexico submitted a "Letter of Intent" to the IMF which presented the economic program for the 1986-1987 biennium. According to the program, $12.5 billion in fresh resources was needed to achieve moderate growth with stability. Additionally, two contingency loans for a total of $2.4 billion were requested. One of these (up to $720 million from the IMF) would be used for facing a possible fall in oil prices to below $9 per barrel. The other loan, for the remaining amount, would be disbursed in the event that growth during the first one-third of 1987 fell short of that forecast.

In September 1986, the IMF decided to support the Mexican program and to disburse $1.7 billion through three-month tranches. The first would be made until the commercial banks decided to contribute 90 percent of the total amount of resources committed to support the Mexican economic program ($6 billion);

this percentage was denoted as the "critical mass." Similarly, the World Bank committed itself to net disbursements of $2.3 billion during 1986-1987.

The negotiations with the commercial banks, in addition to new loans for $6 billion and contingent loans for $1.7 billion, also covered the restructuring of maturities for $52.250 billion, of which 83 percent was contracted for a twenty-year repayment period with a seven-year grace period and a reduction in the surcharge, which was reduced from 1 1/8 points to 13/16 points over the LIBOR. Similarly, $9.7 billion of private debt (with the *Ficorca* scheme) was restructured for twenty years with a seven-year grace period.

Fourth Restructuring, 1988: Toward a New Strategy

Since 1986, mechanisms for reducing the debt through market operations were explored to take advantage of the discounts at which Mexican debt instruments were being quoted on the secondary market. This led to the introduction of a debt for equity conversion (swap) program, which began operating in 1986. On the other hand, toward the beginning of 1988, an exchange of debt for bonds was realized, with U.S. Treasury zero-coupon bonds serving as collateral.[8]

The introduction of the swap program, in addition to reducing the outstanding debt, served to promote foreign investment. The system of substituting public debt for investments was successful, especially since swaps represented approximately 50 percent of all foreign investment authorized by the *Comisión de Inversiones Extranjeras* (Commission of Foreign Investments) in 1986, despite their being introduced in the middle of the year. Via swap operations, $2.126 billion of investments was realized, and simultaneously, $2.488 billion of debt was redeemed.

The other mechanisms used to reduce the outstanding public debt involved the voluntary exchange of the restructured debt for discount bonds, with guaranteed payment of the principal upon maturation (twenty years), through zero-coupon bonds acquired by the Mexican government. The operation took place in February 1988, with the discount at which the exchange would take place to be determined by an auction. The result was a net reduction of the debt in the amount of $1.108 billion and a savings of $1.537 billion in interest that no longer had to be paid during the following twenty years. This operation represented the first time that one of the principal debtor countries used market mechanisms to take advantage of the discount on its debt in the secondary market and gave rise to a new stage in handling the problem of foreign debt.

EFFECTS OF THE EXCESSIVE FOREIGN DEBT ON THE MACROECONOMIC FRAMEWORK

From 1982 to 1988, the total foreign debt rose from $92.408 to $100.384 billion, which on average represented 61 percent of the GDP during this period. In 1986 and 1987, this indicator hit its highest levels ever in Mexican history: 76.3 and 73.6 percent, respectively.

Between 1982 and 1988, payments abroad just to cover interest absorbed an average of 34 percent of the total current account revenues of the balance of payments and in some years represented over 40 percent. This situation could have been worse, but thanks to the restructurings between 1983 and 1987 already described, some $48 billion in payments on principal were deferred for a period of twenty years with a seven-year grace period. Furthermore, fresh resources were obtained, as well as better terms of payment than originally contracted.

As already noted, these restructurings alleviated the strong pressures on the balance of payments. To get an idea of this, it is useful to consider the size of the net transfer of resources abroad due to service payments under the original debt schedule: on average, some $18.7 billion per year between 1983 and 1988. (See Table 1.) This would have been equivalent to 11.4 percent of the GDP, instead of the 6.2 percent observed. It is obvious that to finance payments of such a magnitude would have required an internal adjustment, whose consequences, in terms of social costs, would have been very severe.

Table 1
Effects of the External Public Debt Restructuring Agreements on the Net Transfer of Resources Abroad
(percentage of GDP)

Year	Original Transfer	After the Restructuring
1983	14.4	5.3
1984	10.7	6.6
1985	11.4	6.1
1986	11.5	6.5
1987	12.1	5.5
1988	8.2	6.4

Source: Author's estimate based on information from the Secretaría de Hacienda and Crédito Público and del Banco de México.

Since 1983, simultaneous to the restructurings of the foreign debt, a traditional stabilization policy was implemented. This consisted of controlling aggregate demand. This policy was unavoidable in view of the scarcity of foreign loans and the magnitude of the fiscal and balance of payments deficits, which made it difficult to manage economic policy. Additionally, a medium-term strategy was begun to stimulate economic growth and to endow the economy with greater agility and capacity to adapt to exogenous changes. Within this strategy, the following elements stand out: the process of public sector rationalization, the fiscal reform, the deregulation of the productive apparatus gradually to suppress distortions arising from excessive and generalized price controls, the reduction and elimination of unjustifiable subsidies, a flexible exchange policy, the opening of the economy to foreign trade, and the modernization of the financial system.

In addition to restricting economic growth, the excessive net transfer of resources abroad made the economy extremely vulnerable to external shocks, particularly any deterioration in the terms of trade. Between 1982 and 1988, the terms of trade index fell by about 47 percent. This implied a total loss of revenues on the order of an estimated $40 billion during this period. The deterioration in the terms of trade becomes even worse when the rise in international interest rates is taken into account, in which case, the fall was 53 percent during the same period. These adverse factors made it necessary to extend and intensify the economic stabilization measures.[9]

The stabilization policy was successful: After a deficit of 7 percent of the GDP in 1982, the primary budget balance in 1989 ran a surplus of over 7 percent. On the other hand, the trade balance registered unprecedented surpluses; in 1983 and 1984, Mexico was among the top five countries with the largest surpluses. All of this implied that great efforts had to be made by the country to generate these positive results and thus to service the foreign debt. In other words, resources had to be diverted from consumption and investment, which created recessionary pressures on the economy. If this situation had been maintained, not only would stagnation have been prolonged, but the potential growth of the economy also would have been limited. This would only have aggravated the problem of debt overhang by restricting the country's payment capacity.

In very little time, extraordinary results were observed in the economic realm. Nevertheless, unfavorable events made the full attainment of the goals of the economic stabilization policy impossible: the deterioration in the terms of trade, caused by the contraction in oil prices and the rise in foreign interest rates, and the 1985 earthquakes. The earthquakes had two adverse effects: They increased public expenditure on reconstruction, and they paralyzed the productive apparatus and communications for a number of weeks.

The recent Mexican experience has shown that debt overhang is an obstacle to economic growth. For their part, other cases have demonstrated that the longer a macroeconomic adjustment is postponed, the greater the social cost, since the social cost increases when the adjustment is drastic and can even be dangerous for political stability.

The Mexican experience during these years revealed that the foreign debt crisis was not only a temporary problem arising from liquidity shortages, nor could it be solved by merely granting more credits and deferring payments. That a stabilization policy implies social costs also became evident, as did the need to reduce the cumulative balance on the debt and its service, as well as to assure multiyear financing in order to have enough time for the policies of structural change to take effect. This is the fundamental solution: reducing net transfers of resources abroad.

THE FOREIGN DEBT POLICY DURING 1989-1994
AND THE AGREEMENTS WITH INTERNATIONAL LENDERS

Before beginning this section, it is useful to recall the considerable efforts made during the 1982-1988 period regarding the administration of the public sector foreign debt. Mexico was at the forefront in promoting better and more viable solutions for the foreign debt problem. It should be remembered that after a conjunctural approach, in which the cash flow crisis was seen as only requiring an emphasis on an adjustment program, Mexico began to argue that this type of solution was insufficient for attaining minimum levels of growth and welfare in highly indebted countries. The Baker Plan, proposed in 1985 by the U.S. Secretary of the Treasury, marked the crystallization of a different approach, though still limited, to finding an integral solution to the debt crisis. The guiding principle of the plan was to "grow in order to pay." Nevertheless, the plan had serious limitations, since it did not involve a long-term attack on the problem of net transfers of resources abroad.

Mexico's new approach was viable and was implemented as a negotiating strategy for the 1986-1987 foreign debt. This was possible because other important factors appeared in the international economy and the financial community. Thus, over time, a number of changes took place, both in the creditors' perception of the real problem of highly indebted countries and in the banks' financial situation which made for greater concessions that were not possible at the onset of the crisis. Nevertheless, recognition on the part of the creditors that net foreign transfers were the chief obstacle for future growth did not occur until the end of 1988. At this point, after six years, the banks had created sufficient reserves and, at the same time, recognized that rescheduling the debt profile and granting resources only refueled the problem of net transfers.

In this sense, favorable conditions for changing the perception and the management of the foreign debt did not emerge until 1989. To be in a position to grant concessions that truly reduced the net transfer of resources abroad, as well as the amount of the principal and service payments, the banks needed sufficient reserves and support from their governments. Government support meant fiscal and regulatory measures that would allow the banks to absorb the costs of the concessions granted.

It was evident that Mexico in 1988 could not remain in an economic recession; to do so would be gravely to endanger future growth. Also, the population demanded a reversal in their deteriorating standards of living. To do this, it was imperative to return to economic growth, reduce inflation, and increase the welfare of all Mexicans. For this reason, in his inauguration speech, President Carlos Salinas de Gortari announced that reducing the net transfer of resources abroad to an average level of 2 percent of the GDP between 1989 and 1994 would be one of the chief objectives of the government's economic recovery strategy. In this manner, the government sought to recover Mexico's historical rates of economic growth and reach a rate of growth of 6 percent in 1993 and 1994.

The thrust of the president's foreign debt policy consisted of 1) overcoming the net transfer of resources abroad, 2) assuring multiyear arrangements, 3) reducing the historical value of the foreign debt, and 4) reducing the volume of the debt as a proportion of the GDP.

Thus, toward the end of 1988, talks were initiated with Mexico's different creditors. (As of December 1988, the outstanding Mexican foreign debt rose to $100.384 billion, of which $81.003 billion corresponded to the public sector.) At the same time, all of Mexico's productive sectors signed the first stage of the *Pacto para la Estabilidad y el Crecimiento Económico* (Pact for Stability and Economic Growth), with the firm intent of persevering in the fight against inflation. Mexico, thus, reaffirmed its intention of attaining permanent price stability, through a flexible program which could be adjusted to changes in economic conditions, to avoid shortages of goods and services as well as confrontations between sectors.

Similarly, progress continued to be made in the implementation of the policy of structural change. Toward the end of 1988, the process of trade liberalization was deepened; important changes were announced in the financial sector, and the reduction of the public sector financial deficit from 12.3 percent of the GDP in 1988 to 6 percent in 1989 was established as a public finance objective. On the other hand, reaching a moderate rate of growth that could be sustained over the long term and would preserve the achievements of the stabilization plan also was defined as a goal.

The perception that it was necessary to reduce the foreign debt was not unilateral: Shortly after Salinas' inaugural address, in March 1989, U.S. Treasury Secretary James Brady gave a speech in which he proposed reducing the debt of the developing nations; it was known as the Brady Plan. This was the first positive response to Mexico's position that reducing the transfer of resources abroad was a necessary condition for growth. This proposal represented a departure from positions held prior to the Baker Plan. These,

Table 2
Principal Economic Indicators, 1973-1983

	1973	1974	1975	1976	1977	1978	1979	1980	1981	1982	1983
GDP (real growth)	8.4	6.1	5.6	4.2	3.4	8.2	9.2	8.3	8.8	-0.6	-4.2
Prices (Dec./Dec.)	21.3	20.7	11.2	27.2	20.7	16.2	20.0	29.8	28.7	98.8	80.8
Public financial deficit (as a % of GDP)	6.3	6.7	9.3	9.1	6.3	6.2	7.1	7.5	14.1	16.9	8.6
Terms of exchange	120.8	81.5	73.6	119.7	123.6	113.9	94.3	112.8	126.8	86.1	69.4
Price of oil for export (dollars per barrel)	na	na	na	11.8	13.6	13.2	19.7	31.0	33.2	28.7	26.4

Source: Elaborated by the authors from information obtained from Banco de Mexico and Petróleos Mexicanos.

Table 2, cont.
Principal Economic Indicators, 1984-1993

	1984	1985	1986	1987	1988	1989	1990	1991	1992	1993
GDP (real growth)	3.6	2.6	-3.8	1.7	1.2	3.3	4.4	3.6	2.6	0.4
Prices (Dec./Dec.)	59.2	63.7	105.7	159.2	51.7	19.7	29.9	18.8	11.9	8.0
Public financial deficit (as a % of GDP)	8.5	9.6	15.9	16.0	12.4	5.5	3.5	1.5	-1.7	-1.0
Terms of exchange	70.8	72.4	52.9	67.0	60.5	64.5	67.9	65.0	63.9	62.1
Price of oil for export (dollars per barrel)	26.8	25.3	11.9	16.0	12.2	15.6	19.2	14.6	14.8	13.2

Source: Elaborated by the authors from information obtained from Banco de Mexico and Petróleos Mexicanos.

basically, centered on granting fresh loans to the indebted countries. Later, in the first days of April, the countries of the Group of Seven gave their support to the Brady Plan.

A decisive element in the foreign debt negotiation process was the signing, on March 26, 1989, by the IMF and the Mexican government of an Extended Fund Facility Arrangement for three years, with the Mexican government retaining an option for a fourth year. For the first time, the IMF backed an economic program with a fundamental objective of economic growth. In contrast to previous agreements traditionally subscribed by the IMF, which limited public spending by restricting financial resources without regard for the accompanying recessionary effects, this arrangement placed the goal of economic growth as the premise from which financing requirements would follow.

The announcement of the Brady Plan, the signing of the agreement with the IMF, and the explicit support of the principal Organization for Economic Cooperation and Development (OECD) countries, as well as the agreement reached with the World Bank for financial support, were indications of international recognition of the economic policy adjustments being made by Mexico, as well as of the undeniable need to reduce the burden of the debt. In this context, conditions for negotiating with the commercial banks improved.

On May 26, 1989, the IMF Executive Board unanimously approved the letter of intent presented by Mexico. The approval established that Mexico would have at its disposal $4.135 billion to be disbursed over each trimester until February 1992. Similarly, it was agreed that part of these resources would be used to support debt reduction operations proposed by Mexico to its creditor banks.

An arrangement was signed with the World Bank on June 13, 1989, to grant Mexico loans for a total of $1.960 billion during 1989. These funds would be used to carry out investment projects in the energy, industrial, financial, commercial, and public sectors. Of this amount, $375 million was to be dedicated to debt reduction operations with the commercial banks (described below). Also, it was agreed that an average of $2 billion a year in credits would be granted during the 1990-1992 period.

With the Paris Club, made up of financial representatives from sixteen industrialized countries, Mexico attained a multiyear agreement for $2.6 billion in bilateral credit lines. This amount represented all of the principal maturing between June 1, 1989, and March 31, 1992, as well as 100 percent of the interest falling due between June 1, 1989, and March 31, 1990, 90 percent of the interest due between April 1, 1990, and March 31, 1991, and 80 percent of the interest due between April 1, 1991, and May 25, 1992. The agreement also provided for certainty regarding the availability of financing for Mexican imports from Paris Club members. These were calculated at, at least, $2 billion a year between 1989 and 1994.

Negotiations with the commercial banks were formally initiated on April 19, 1989. Most of Mexico's public sector foreign debt was and is contracted with these banks. As of this date, the outstanding foreign debt with the commercial banks was approximately $52.6 billion, an amount which constituted the so-called outstanding amount eligible for restructuring. Nevertheless, in the course of 1989, a number of operations were effected that reduced the outstanding debt to nearly $48 billion. These operations were 1) redemption of the public sector foreign debt that some official institutions held as payment for the sale of quasi-official firms that were privatized, 2) debt for equity swaps authorized prior to November 1987, 3) net repayment by the public sector during 1989, and 4) variations in the exchange rate of the dollar with other currencies.

After a long process of negotiations, on July 23, 1989, an "agreement in principle" was reached with the commercial banks allowing them to choose among the following alternatives: 1) exchange debt for new bonds at a 35 percent discount, "discount bonds," paying LIBOR plus 13/16 of a point; 2) exchange debt for new bonds with the same original value but at a fixed 6.25 percent interest rate, known as "par bonds"; or 3) grant new loans, "new money," for an amount equal to 25 percent of the nominal value of the debt not assigned to either of the first two options, to be distributed over a four-year period in the following manner: 7 percent in 1989; 6 percent per year from 1990 through 1992. The interest rate for this new money would be LIBOR plus 13/16 of a point, with a fifteen-year repayment and a seven-year grace period. The banks could choose one alternative or a combination of them. This choice basically depended on each bank's financial position, the fiscal and legal dispositions in each country, and their assessment of future "Mexico risk."

For the first two alternatives, it was agreed to extend the repayment period from twenty years with a seven-year grace period to thirty years with a single payment at the termination of the period. The repayment of the principal would be fully backed by Mexico's acquisition of zero-coupon bonds from the treasuries of the United States and other countries. These would mature after thirty years. Additionally, Mexico would deposit an amount to guarantee payment of eighteen months of interest on the new bonds. These resources would not imply an additional net cost, since, as investments, they generated interest for Mexico in an amount similar to the interest to be paid on them.

The alternatives presented to the banks by Mexico were drawn with the objective of meeting the macroeconomic restriction that net transfers abroad be reduced to an annual average of less than 2 percent during the 1989-1994 period and that, for the banks, these be equivalent in terms of their net present value adjusted for risk (PVAR).

When the banks feel that income flows are free of risk, they discount at the market rate. If this isn't the case, they discount at a higher rate, thereby reflecting the "Mexico risk." For a formalization of this important aspect of the negotiations with the commercial banks, see Appendix 2.[10] Using a 15 percent discount rate for nonbacked flows (the "new money" alternative and the component of nonbacked interest payments in the first two alternatives), the three alternatives implied a PVAR of approximately 35 percent of the value of the previously restructured debt, whereas just prior to the signing of the agreement in principle with the commercial banks, the price of Mexican debt instruments on the secondary market was around forty-one cents per dollar.

Other important points in the package were the following:

1. The realization of a $3.5 billion debt for equity swap program to be used to finance infrastructure projects and to acquire up to 50 percent of the value of shares of public firms being privatized. The objective of the latter was to avoid any possible inflationary effects of the swap program.

2. The inclusion of a contingency clause in the event of a fall in oil prices, which stipulated that if oil prices fell below $10 per barrel (in 1989 prices), a group of commercial banks, the World Bank, and the IMF will contribute about $1 billion to compensate. It should be pointed out that, in practice, this clause has already been surpassed, since the Mexican government has created its own contingency fund with the 1990 oil export surplus, as well as income from the sale of public firms.

3. The inclusion of a value recovery clause, according to which, if the price of Mexican export oil rises above fourteen real 1989 dollars per barrel, and, if and only if, the total revenue from oil exports in real terms is higher than the revenue obtained in 1989, Mexico will increase the interest on the "par" and "discount" bonds in an amount not to exceed 30 percent of the additional oil income. This increase will be weighted according to the ratio of debt involved in the reduction alternatives and will have as a cap maximum earnings of an additional 3 percent annually.

4. The "financial package" grants Mexico the legal flexibility to realize direct repurchases of the reduction bonds and to carry out debt exchanges for debt or for equity when they are to Mexico's advantage.

Table 3

Estimate of the Return on Reduction Bonds for the Recapture of Oil Income in 1996, with Different Assumptions Regarding the "Going" Price

Nominal agreed price (dollars per barrel)	14.00	14.00	14.00	14.00	14.00	14.00	14.00	14.00	14.00	14.00
Deflator for growth rate	40.71	40.71	40.71	40.71	40.71	40.71	40.71	40.71	40.71	40.71
Adjusted reference price (dollars per barrel)	19.70	19.70	19.70	19.70	19.70	19.70	19.70	19.70	19.70	19.70
Going price (dollars per barrel)	20.00	21.00	22.00	23.00	24.00	25.00	26.00	27.00	28.00	30.20
Cumulative growth viz 1989	25.00	31.25	37.50	43.75	50.00	56.25	62.50	68.75	75.00	88.75
Relative price of oil	0.89	0.93	0.98	1.02	1.07	1.11	1.15	1.20	1.24	1.34
Volume of exports (millions of barrels per day)	1.25	1.25	1.25	1.25	1.25	1.25	1.25	1.25	1.25	1.25
Total oil revenue (billions of dollars)	9.13	9.58	10.04	10.49	10.95	11.41	11.86	12.32	12.78	13.78
Debt eligible for reduction (billions of dollars)	48.00	48.00	48.00	48.00	48.00	48.00	48.00	48.00	48.00	48.00
Proportion of reduction bonds	0.91	–	0.91	–	0.91	–	0.91	–	0.91	0.91
Payments for additional income	37.36	161.64	285.92	410.21	534.49	658.77	783.05	907.34	1031.62	1305.04
Payments/balance for reduction of debt	0.09	0.37	0.66	0.94	1.23	1.51	1.80	2.08	2.37	2.99
Oil payments/ income from petroleum	0.004	0.017	0.029	0.039	0.049	0.058	0.066	0.074	0.081	0.095

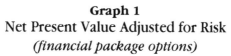

Graph 1
Net Present Value Adjusted for Risk
(financial package options)

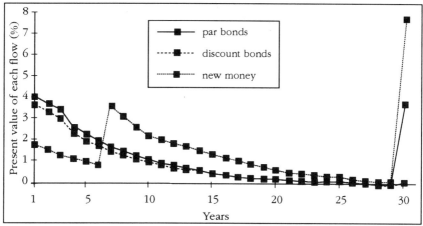

As an example, the value recovery clause will work in the following manner: In the event that the growth of the price deflator of the U.S. GDP is 5 percent per year on average between 1989 and 1996, the real posted price of oil would be $19.7 per barrel (the equivalent of fourteen 1989 dollars). However, if the price prevailing in 1996 is $22 (see column 3 of Table 3), Mexico would make additional payments to its creditors of $286 million in 1996, that is, 0.66 percent of the base debt that had been exchanged for reduction bonds.

On March 28, 1990, the exchange of the old debt for the new instruments took place in New York. The distribution selected by the banks of the eligible $48.086 billion was as follows: 1) 42.8 percent of this balance was exchanged for "discount" bonds, 2) 46.64 percent was exchanged for "par" bonds, 3) 9.12 percent served as the basis for supplying new money, and 4) the remaining 1.44 percent corresponded to Facilities 2 and 3 contained in the 1986-1987 restructuring agreement, which were not subject to change in this last negotiation.

Since the disbursement of loans to Mexico for the formation of guarantees was realized in stages until 1992, a group of commercial banks granted a letter of credit that allowed Mexico to cover all of the guarantees by the date specified in the agreement with the commercial lenders. As the disbursements from official sources were received between 1990 and 1992, the letter of credit would be canceled; for this reason, the final contribution of the EximBank of Japan rose to $2.05 billion.

Table 4
Contribution of Resources for Guarantees
(millions of dollars)

Total	7122.1
International Monetary Fund	1268.3
World Bank	2010.0
EximBank, Japan	1380.2
Federal Government	1373.6
Letter of Credit	1090.0

Once the old debt had been exchanged for the new bonds, the outstanding public foreign debt was reduced by $7.203 billion, as a result of the exchange for "discount" bonds. In terms of foreign exchange flows, the direct benefits accruing from the agreement with the commercial banks rose to an annual average of $3.673 billion for the period 1990-1994. This amount breaks down into the following components: 1) a savings in interest, arising from the first two alternatives, in the amount of $1.301 billion ($657 million of which correspond to the discount option and $644 million to the reduction in interest rates);[11] 2) payments on principal for $2.154 billion, which no longer

Graph 2
Reduction of External Transfers
Financial Package 1989-1992
(millions of dollars)

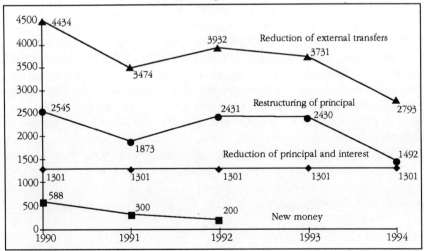

Source: Ministry of Treasury and Public Credit.

had to be paid by Mexico since the new debt bonds have a thirty-year term and will be paid upon maturity with the zero-coupon bonds acquired; and 3) new loans in an average amount of $218 million per year during the period ($588 million in 1990, $300 million in 1991, and $200 million in 1992).

EVALUATION OF THE BENEFITS OF RESTRUCTURING

An evaluation of the benefits derived from the financial package must examine a variety of aspects in addition to foreign exchange savings and the entry of new loans. On the one hand, it must be determined whether the resources for the guarantees were efficiently used in comparison with, for example, a direct repurchase of the debt on the secondary market. On the other, it must be specified whether the objectives posed were achieved, in light of the premises that guided the renegotiation of the debt. It is appropriate then to ask whether the reduction of net external transfers in the magnitude obtained is sufficient for reinitiating economic growth.

Regarding the first point, upon evaluating the restructuring agreement as an investment project, with an initial disbursement equivalent to the constitution of the guarantees, following the methodology proposed by Van Wijnbergen (1990), the internal rate of return is approximately 37 percent, which exceeds by fourfold the cost of the resources for the acquisition of these guarantees.[12] Net income is given by the difference between the sum of 1) the savings on the service of the old debt, 2) the freeing up of the guarantees that don't have to be used, 3) the grants of new money, and 4) the interest accruing to Mexico from the deposit for eighteen months of the guarantee interest minus the sum of 1) the service on the new instruments and 2) the total amount of the guarantees. This estimate assumes a LIBOR of 10 percent (with the 13/16 point surcharge already included) and an estimate of the flows already indicated, compatible with the final distribution of the original debt among the alternatives of the financial package.

The reduction of net transfers abroad that resulted from the agreement implied less pressure on the exchange rate. This reduced the risk associated with the domestic public debt and, therefore, induced a drop in real interest rates. This created a virtual circle: confidence — lower interest rates — less public deficit — control over inflation — more confidence. Just one month after the agreement with the principal lending bank, the nominal interest rates declined by nearly 20 percentage points, precisely as a result of greater confidence. This not only represented an incentive for productive investment; it also contributed to alleviating public finances considerably: Given the outstanding domestic public debt at that moment, a reduction of 20 percentage points translated into a savings of approximately 1,960 billion old pesos per month ($796 million). Thus, if the savings in interest on the domestic debt as an indirect result of the restructuring arrangement are taken into account, the internal rate of return goes from 37 percent to 65 percent.[13]

However, if the resources for the guarantees had been utilized to effect direct repurchase operations and obtain all of the discount offered by the secondary market, the results would have been as follows: Assuming a price of 50 cents per dollar of debt, only $14.244 billion of debt could have been purchased with $7.122 billion. Still, another $5.748 billion would have to be discounted from this reduction for the credits obtained to constitute the guarantees; this results in a net reduction of $8.496 billion, which would have implied a discount of only 17.7 percent on the original balance. Nevertheless, Mexico would not have obtained the reduction of interest rates from the market level to a fixed 6.25 percent on the amount of $22.427 billion. This also represented a reduction of approximately $7.2 billion.[14] It should also be stressed that the secondary debt market is extremely thin and that the operations made in it are for relatively small amounts. Thus, a program of repurchases of the magnitude indicated would have led to a considerable increase in prices, which would have made such an operation only marginally profitable.

As to the second point, the benefits of the restructuring of the foreign public debt translated into a substantial reduction in net transfers of resources abroad. Here, the initial goal (an average 2 percent of the GDP per year for the 1990-1994 period) was surpassed considerably, since, in addition to the reduction obtained from restructuring the debt, the change in the expectations of economic agents following the negotiations resulted in capital inflows. From 1989 to 1992, net transfers of resources abroad ceased, and Mexico once again became a net recipient of capital, at an average annual rate of 3.3 percent of its GDP. This flow of resources toward the country has contributed to covering the economy's financial requirements.

The reactivation of the economy and the reduction of the outstanding debt and its service have combined to cause a considerable positive change in the indicators of Mexico's creditworthiness. The total outstanding foreign debt represented 30.8 percent of the GDP in 1992, a figure 32.2 percentage points below the 1983-1988 average and 45.5 percentage points below the maximum level for the period (76.3 percent), which was registered in 1986. In 1992, Mexico's outstanding foreign debt was 1.7 times greater than current account income, whereas from 1983 through 1988 it was, on average, 3.2 times the current account income. For their part, payments on total foreign interest as a proportion of current account income declined from 31.2 percent on average per year between 1983 and 1988 to 12.7 percent in 1992; if this is related to the GDP, there is a fall from 6.0 percent to 2.3 percent for the same years.

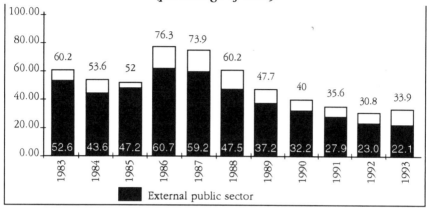

Graph 3
Total External Debt 1983-1993
(percentage of GDP)

Source: Ministry of Treasury and Public Credit.

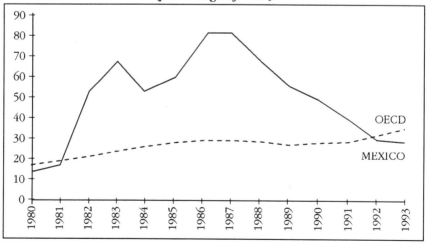

Graph 4
Variations in the Balance of Net Total Public Debt
Comparison Mexico/OECD* 1980-1993
(percentage of GDP)

*Includes all OECD member countries except Mexico.
Sources: OECD and Ministry of Treasury and Public Credit.

Table 5

	Mexico	Spain	Portugal	Greece	Turkey
External debt/GDP	33.00%	20.00%	45.00%	60.00%	50.00%
External debt/exports	180.00%	90.00%	130.00%	230.00%	230.00%
Debt service/exports	11.00%	5.00%	8.00%	15.00%	12.00%
Current account/GDP	-6.00%	-2.00%	-0.50%	-1.50%	-4.60%

The conjunction of direct and indirect effects has contributed to the fulfillment of the present administration's principal economic policy objective of returning to economic growth with stable prices. During the 1989-1992 period, the GDP grew at an average real rate of 3.5 percent, although in 1993 the GDP grew by only 0.4 percent. It should be pointed out that, although growth has been slower than expected, it contrasts considerably from the average observed in 1982-1988: 0 percent. The fact that the GDP has grown on average 2.9 percent over the 1989-1993 period in an international context of recession and with strict controls on inflation is a sign of the notable improvement in the Mexican economy's potential. Inflation fell from 19.7 percent and 29.9 percent in 1989 and 1990, respectively, to 8 percent in 1993. Certainty regarding the evolution of the economy, the debt renegotiation allowed for a deepening and broadening of the economic stabilization and reform policies served as a catalyst for the economic program.

According to the econometric estimates of Van Wijnbergen (1990), the combined effect of a reduction in net external transfers, the reduction in real internal interest rates, and the greater confidence among agents explains about two percentage points of GDP growth during the 1989-1994 period.[15]

Another advantage of the new structure of the public sector bank foreign debt is that $22.426 billion, which was previously contracted at a floating interest rate (LIBOR plus 13/16 of a percentage point), is now subject to a fixed rate of 6.25 percent, or its equivalent in other currencies. This means that the Mexican economy is much less vulnerable to variations in international interest rates — that rose to around 20 percent at the beginning of the 1980s — over which Mexico has no control.

ADMINISTRATION OF THE FOREIGN DEBT, 1989-1994
Participation of Voluntary Capital Markets

The restructuring of the debt has also had important repercussions on the quality and availability of external resources for Mexico. The costs of loans have gradually declined due to a perception of less risk in the country. The sale of public and private debt on the voluntary capital markets has become an ever more important source of financing. Gaining access to these markets has occurred gradually, with diversification to avoid saturation.

The strategy of reentry into these markets has consisted of issuing bonds for public sector entities in different markets, which has served as an opening for private sector issues. Although the markets in dollars have been the most important source of resources, issues have also been realized in German marks, Spanish *pesetas*, and British pounds sterling. In September 1992, the first issue, called the Yankee Bond, was realized in the U.S. market, thereby opening the door to the largest financial market in the world. It should be remembered that *Bancomext* (*Banco Nacional de Comercio Exterior*, National Bank of Foreign Trade) was the first to reenter the voluntary capital markets in 1989, at a crucial moment favorable to the foreign debt negotiations. *Pemex* initiated the entry into the market for commercial papers, as well as the Austrian, European Currency Unit (ECU), and Japanese bond markets. From June 1989 to August 1993, the public sector placed bonds for a total of $6.268 billion, while the private sector placed $7.960 billion. It is worth noting that despite the importance of Mexico's return to the voluntary capital markets, it will always be necessary to utilize this source of resources prudently to finance activities that give rise to net benefits in the long run.

Table 6
Sale of Public Sector Bonds, 1989-1993

Year	Number of Issues	Amount ($ millions)
1989	2	420
1990	9	792
1991	16	1835
1992	8	1020
1993	33	3753

Source: Secretaría de Hacienda y Crédito Público.

As subsequent public and private sector issuances were realized, over the past three years terms have become more and more favorable, particularly in regard to interest rates and, more importantly, the size of spreads. Access to voluntary capital markets was facilitated by the ratings given to Mexican debt instruments by the international rating agencies. In 1990, Moody's Investor's Service gave the long-term sovereign debt an intermediate rating of "speculative grade" (Ba 2), whereas in 1992 Standard and Poor's Ratings (S&P) gave it a grade of "BB+," which is the best speculative grade, one notch below "investment grade."[16]

These ratings were lower than expected; in fact, the authors of this article openly expressed their disagreement with the ratings and the criteria used.

Furthermore, these agencies systematically rank debtors below the levels that they themselves consider to be correct. This is done as a strategy to avoid having to make downward corrections when necessary, since such adjustments could lead to a loss of credibility among investors regarding these agencies' capacities to evaluate risks. An upward adjustment, on the other hand, would not have this effect. Causing particular surprise are the variables that are given most weight and the extremely short-term vision of the rating agencies' analyses. As a sign that the markets "know" more than any erudite analysis, within weeks of the first rating, prices on the Mexican debt rose considerably in the secondary market. This occurred since most institutional investors, by their statutes, are obligated to hold only rated assets in their portfolios. Thus, once the Mexican debt was ranked, the market placed the Mexico risk at its proper level. Similarly, the September 1992 placement or issue of the Yankee Bond was effected with a 8.5 percent coupon (with a ten-year term); at the time, this rate of return was very similar to that paid by bonds of countries ranked as investment grade.[17] It should be stressed that in December 1992 Standard and Poor's granted Mexico the highest grade that it gives to short-term domestic public debt in national currency (in this case, Cetes). This contributed to increasing foreign demand for these bonds.

Public Debt for Equity Swap Program

During 1990, in fulfillment of one of the clauses of the financial package, the Program of Exchanging Public Debt for Equity was carried out for $3.5 billion of the value of the original debt participating in the package. The use of swaps was restricted to financing infrastructure projects and the acquisition of up to 50 percent of the value of shares of some of the public enterprises being privatized. The program was open both to the participating banks and to national and foreign investors. The debt eligible for participation in the program was the recently restructured debt, that is to say, discount bonds, par bonds (the base of new money), and new money. The swaps were carried out using the auction system. This was done to capture the greatest discount possible and to make the assignment of exchange rates more overt. To this effect, an intersecretarial committee was formed, which was in charge of defining the details of the two auctions to be held in 1990, as well as the evaluation of proposed investment projects.

Given the large demand for exchange rights, the single discount rate for both auctions was situated around 52 percent, a rate similar to that observed on the secondary market. The program remained in force until April 1992. As of that date, the amount of exchange rights exercised was only $600 million (37 percent of the amount assigned), which allowed for the redemption of $813 million in foreign public debt.[18] This amount, which was less than the amount included in the program, occurred because during 1991, the use of swaps was inhibited by an increase in the price of Mexican debt instruments on the secondary market. This rise was due to the favorable evolution of the economy, the clear improvement in Mexico's creditworthiness, and the already mentioned fact that the sovereign Mexican debt had already met the requirement of being graded by internationally recognized agencies.

Given the size of the discount obtained in the two auctions, the present value of the service on the domestic debt issued when effecting the conversion — in a context of gradually falling internal interest rates — was considerably less than the service corresponding to the foreign debt canceled. This implied an important reduction of the cost of the total public sector foreign debt.

In mid-1990, by a unilateral decision of the Mexican government, a special program of swaps dedicated to education, health, and ecology, among other areas, was initiated. This program, which is still in effect, operates on the basis of donations (as a necessary condition) received by nonprofit institutions. The special treatment consists of redeeming the nominal value of the debt and granting the total profit from the exchange to the institution executing the project. This profit results from the difference in the price of the debt bonds on the secondary market and their nominal value. From July 1990 to September 30, 1992, 98 social swap projects were authorized for a nominal amount of $704 million. Of the amount authorized, $300 million (42 percent of the total) corresponds to education; $203 million (29 percent), to urban development and the environment; $195 million (28 percent), to social welfare; and $5.5 million (1 percent), to agriculture and livestock.

Leveraged Repurchases of Debt

The 1989-1992 financial package provides the legal flexibility for Mexico to effect direct repurchases of the restructured debt and to carry out debt for debt exchanges, whenever advantageous to Mexico. Since the second half of 1990, Mexico has carried out repurchases of debt on the secondary market, thereby continuing to reduce the historic outstanding debt, principally through "leveraged repurchases." This method consists of obtaining resources for the repurchases by contracting loans with the commercial banks or by issuing bonds, providing as guarantee the very bonds repurchased; these are repaid until the loan requested is repaid.[19] An important advantage of the leveraged repurchases is that they avoid the use of the country's international reserves.[20]

On June 1, 1992, the Secretary of Finance, Pedro Aspe, announced a $7.171 billion reduction in the outstanding foreign public debt. This resulted from the repayment of the loans used between 1990 and the first half of 1992 for repurchases and the subsequent cancellation of the discount bonds that were held as guarantees. The resources for repaying the loans used between 1990 and June 1992 came from the ones contracted from banks and from bonds, as well as from the sale of a second package of shares in *Telmex*, which was still federal government property. Thus, on the basis of transitory, nonrecurring income arising from the privatization of public firms, a permanent benefit was obtained: the reduction of the foreign debt.

The cancellation of $7.171 billion of debt is equivalent to a reduction of 9 percent of the outstanding foreign public debt as of March 31, 1992, and to approximately 2.2 percent of the 1992 GDP. Other important benefits are the savings in interest payments — estimated at $654 million a year — and the savings that would result in the event of application of the value recovery clause agreed to in the 1989-1992 financial package.

Restructuring of Interbank Facilities

In 1991, the federal government decided to hold an auction to exchange liabilities (known as interbank facilities) for new bank privatization bonds, issued by the federal government.[21] As of July 1991, the amount of these facilities was $3.776 billion with a renewal commitment that expired on December 31, 1992.

The amount of the privatization bonds to be auctioned was fixed at $1 billion. These would be exchanged for the interbank facilities. The bonds possessed the following characteristics: a ten-year repayment period with a five-and-a-half-year grace period, at an annual rate of LIBOR at three months plus 13/16 of a point. The principal feature of these bonds was that they could be used as a means of payment (at par) for the acquisition of the Mexican banks in the process of privatization.[22]

The auction was held on July 3, 1991, with 32 lending banks participating with 67 bids, which offered a total of $1.170 billion in interbank facilities. In accordance with the average discount offered of 1.56 percent, this gave rise to an issuance equivalent to $1.151 billion in privatization bonds. As a result of this operation, the foreign debt was reduced by $1.170 billion. Of this amount, $19 million corresponded to the discount captured in the auction, whereas $1.151 billion corresponded to the privatization bonds that were used to acquire shares in the banks being privatized. Additionally, the universe of interbank facilities was reduced by about 31 percent; this corresponded to the most volatile and unstable part of these liabilities. The banks that had the greatest share of interbank facilities among their liabilities were the banks that achieved the greatest reduction. Finally, with the exchange liabilities obtained by the federal government in the operation, Mexico proceeded to redeem ahead of time long-term debt held by the federal government with Mexican banks, thereby enhancing the banks' balances and their value, with the goal of facilitating the process of privatization.[23]

Administration of Risk

As part of the strategy to improve Mexico's financial solvency, in addition to seeking to reduce the historic outstanding debt and reduce net external transfers, the government has explored and participated in new financial markets through the use of products for reducing risk.

Toward the end of 1991, a program of hedging risks was initiated which protects part of the foreign public debt contracted at a floating rate from increases in international interest rates. Presently, the program of hedging offers protection until 1995.

In general terms, there are two types of instruments to hedge the risk of interest rates: 1) agreements on future rates and swaps or exchanges of floating rates for a fixed rate and 2) interest rate options (caps and floors) and options on exchanges of floating rates for a fixed rate (swaptions) that permit fixing the maximum rate at which the debt will be serviced, maintaining for the country the advantage of paying a lower interest rate if the prevailing market rate is lower than the maximum rate fixed in the hedging contract.

The administration of risk with this measure reduces the vulnerability of the economy to adverse external events, as well as makes it possible to plan expenditures with greater precision, since the rate — or the range of fluctuation — of service on an important part of the public sector foreign debt is known beforehand.

CONCLUSIONS

At present, it can be asserted that Mexico has overcome its problem of foreign debt overhang and that, supported by a solid and efficient economic policy, Mexico is ready to initiate a new stage of expansion with low rates of inflation, in which national and foreign investment replace foreign loans as the principal source of development financing.

The permanent solution to the problem of debt overhang required a process of maturation. Both the application of a firm adjustment policy — which led to the establishment of basic macroeconomic equilibria — as well as the earlier restructurings of the foreign debt granted the time and room for maneuver to make viable the search for a permanent solution without breaking with the international financial community, an alternative that undoubtedly would have been extremely prejudicial for Mexico.

The considerable reduction of net external transfers as a proportion of the GDP was possible only by means of voluntary operations to reduce the balance of and service on the foreign debt and by contributions of fresh money; nevertheless, a necessary condition for doing this was the creation of sufficient reserves on the part of the commercial banks and fiscal support from their governments. It was also necessary for creditors and debtors to become aware that this was the road to a permanent solution to the problem of debt overhang.

The benefits of the financial package have not been limited to its effect on the balance of payments and the exchange rate. There are other very important indirect effects that have already appeared. Among these, the strengthening of confidence among economic agents stands out. This induced a fall in real interest rates from a high of 45 percent in July 1989 to 4.4 percent in 1992.

The reduction of real interest rates has had favorable effects on other areas of the economy. For example, they have led to a reduction in the size of the service on the domestic public debt which, along with permanent public financial discipline and the continuous effort at structural change and economic modernization, has made it possible to continue reducing the public sector fiscal deficit, to the point of obtaining a financial surplus of 1 percent in 1993, congruent with the objective of reducing inflation to international levels.

On the other hand, since the announcement of the agreement in principle with the commercial banks through August 1993, repatriations of capital were registered in the amount of about $11.3 billion. Similarly, direct foreign investment from the inauguration of President Salinas in December 1988 through December 1993 reached $23.843 billion. If portfolio investments are included, the total foreign investment increases to $41.741 billion; this figure quadruples the goal targeted for the end of the Salinas administration. Another significant effect has been Mexico's return to the international capital markets after a number of years on their margins. In 1993 alone, 77 bond issues for $7.643 billion were realized by the public and private sectors. These issues were effected under ever more favorable conditions for Mexico, thus demonstrating that the "country risk" has lessened.

For the resources freed by the debt restructuring to translate effectively into sustained economic growth, the creation of new employment, and an increase in the welfare of the population, it will be necessary to continue with and persist in the efforts at economic adjustment, modernization, and structural change already reached. It should be remembered that the goal of reducing transfers of resources abroad is inscribed within a broader strategy.

Notes

1. Oil exports represented 5 percent of the GDP in 1979-1981, whereas they averaged 1.6 percent during 1977-1978. However, the real magnitude of growth of public spending and the sluggishness of other sources of income more than compensated for the abundance of oil revenues.

2. Due to the appreciation of the real exchange rate during these years, the growth of external interest as a proportion of GDP is not revealed in its full magnitude. To put in context the real magnitude of interest payments, it is sufficient to note that the ratio of interest payments to total current account income increased from 21.5 percent in 1977 to 34 percent in 1981.

3. Interest payments continued to be realized in full. Similarly, the deferral did not include 1) direct loans guaranteed by government agencies granting loans for exports, 2) loans from official institutions, 3) government bonds, 4) certain commercial financing, and 5) the private sector debt.

4. The service on the private debt was practically interrupted during the last four months of 1982 and the first months of 1983, giving rise to an accumulation of arrears on interest of about $900 million.

5. A repayment period of ten years with a five-and-a-half-year grace period was agreed to, at an interest rate of LIBOR plus 1 1/2 points or the prime rate plus 1 1/8 points; the commission was 5/8 percent.

6. The net transfer of resources abroad is defined as the amount of resources that results from the current account balance minus the balance of the factor service balance (excluding payments to the labor factor), minus the net change in international reserves.

7. The indicators commonly used to measure a country's foreign debt overhang, in addition to the ratio net external transfers/GDP, are interest payments as a percentage of exports and the outstanding debt as a percentage of exports.

8. Zero-coupon bonds are long-term (from ten to thirty years) investment instruments. They are so named because they do not pay interest in exchange for a coupon as is usually the case; rather, earnings are continuously reinvested, and there is a single final payment of principal and interest. The rate of interest is fixed at the moment of purchase and does not vary. These bonds are commonly issued by government treasuries and are considered to be highly trustworthy.

9. The identities of national accounts provide a simple manner to establish the relationship between growth and the net transfer of resources. The identity of investment, understood as the sum of the gross fixed capital formation (I) and investment in inventory (Inv.), is as follows:

$$I + Inv. = (Sp + D) + Sg + [(M-X) + TF]$$

where Sp = private savings, D = depreciation, Sg = government savings, M = imports, X = exports, TF = net income arising from the rest of the world. This implies that productive investment is financed through domestic and/or foreign savings represented by the term [(M-X) + TF], which for practical purposes can be identified with the balance of payments current account. It follows then that if resources are transferred abroad, financing for investment declines, and, therefore, the potential for stable growth deteriorates. Thus, it becomes clear why Mexico, in its strategy of foreign debt restructuring in 1989-1990, set the reduction of net transfers abroad as a necessary condition for generating growth with price stability.

10. The introduction of the concept of economic value to evaluate the alternatives presented to the banks casts a unique angle upon the negotiation process, facilitating the agreements reached.

11. Estimates of the savings arising from interest payments were based on a LIBOR of 8.31 percent, which was the average annual rate in effect from 1970 to 1991, plus the 13/16 point surcharge that Mexico pays on the restructured debt.

12. This estimate is very similar to that of Van Wiljnbergen (36 percent).

13. A conservative difference between observed and expected interest rates for 1991, which probably would have occurred without the agreement, was used in making this estimate. The assumed difference was 4 percentage points for the second half of 1989, 3 percentage points for the first half of 1990, 2 percentage points for the second half and 1 percentage point for the first half of 1991; beginning with the second half of 1991, equivalent interest rates were presupposed with or without the restructuring. Using the formula [(1+i)/(1+e)-1], in which i is the internal interest rate in pesos and e is the devaluation for the period, the dollar difference in rates was obtained. This, applied to a domestic debt of $53 billion, generated a flow of savings, resulting from the fall in internal interest rates, which when added to the flows considered in the first exercise gives rise to the indicated increase in the internal rate of return implicit in the agreement.

14. The implicit reduction of $7.2 billion results from estimating the present value of interest payments that would have had to be made on the outstanding balance involved in the interest rate reduction alternative, assuming a LIBOR of 8.31 percent.

15. In the simulation exercise carried out by the authors, the absence of a restructuring package with the commercial banks would have obligated the Mexican government to reduce public spending on investment in order to be able to continue servicing the public debt; real interest rates would have remained at a level of 30 percent per year (which was the average value over the twelve months prior to the signing of the agreement), discouraging private investment. The decline in public and private investment would have had a negative impact on the rate of growth, estimated at around one percentage point initially, but it would reach over two percentage points in 1994, when the collateral effects of the destabilization of the exchange rate, in the absence of foreign financing, are added to the decline in investment. This meant that, as a result of the international economic recession, the Mexican economy would have experienced zero or negative rates of growth in 1992 and 1993.

16. Speculative grade is given to debt that is considered to be vulnerable, which faces greater uncertainty or risks arising from adverse economic or financial conditions that might result in inadequate capacity duly to cancel principal and interest payments.

The correspondence between the Moody's and S&P nomenclature for speculative grade is as follows:

Moody's	S&P
Ba 1	BB+
Ba 2	BB
Ba 3	BB-

17. The Yankee Bond was sold at a price of $99.75, thereby offering the investor an 8.62 percent return.

18. The degree of fulfillment of the swap program was 32.14 percent; this results from dividing 813 by 2,529. The latter figure is the value of the original $3.5 billion after the reduction agreements, that is, including the 35 percent reduction of the discount bonds that some of the bidders offered in the two auctions.

19. The object of leaving the repurchased debt as collateral is to obtain better cost and repayment conditions in the repurchase contracts.

20. Thus, paradoxically, at the beginning of the process, there is an increase in the outstanding debt and a net reduction of the debt only once all credits and the repurchased bonds left as a guarantee are repaid.

21. The interbank facilities are short-term deposits (between a week and six months) effected by international banks in Mexican banks that have agencies abroad.

22. The foreign banks had three options: 1) Sell the new bonds to investors interested in acquiring bank stock; 2) acquire this stock themselves, within the limits defined by law; and/or 3) hold the bonds until maturation. This last option was of little interest to holders of interbank facilities principally because of the difference in periods and in liquidity. The whole exercise was slanted in favor of option 1.

23. The Mexican banks had lent part of the resources procured through the interbank facilities — whose average maturation period was less than 90 days — to the federal government, but for a much longer period. This gap in terms left the Mexican commercial banks in a very vulnerable position. With the "catch" described, the problem was reduced considerably.

REFERENCES

Banco de Mexico. *Informe Anual.* Various numbers.

Córdoba, José. 1991. "Diez lecciones de la reforma economica Mexicana." *Nexos*(158).

Dornbusch, Rudiger. 1990. *La Reducción de las Transferencias de los Países Deudores.* México, D.F.: El Trimestre Económico.

El-Khouri, Samir. 1990. "La Restructuración de la Deuda: Experiencia reciente de Mexico." Washington, D.C.: International Monetary Fund. May.

Fischer, Stanley. 1988. "Economic Development and the Debt Crisis." World Bank Working Papers, June. Washington, D.C.

García de Alba, P., and J. Serra Puche. 1984. *Causas y Efectos de la Crisis Económica en México.* México, D.F.: El Colegio de México.

Gurría, José A. 1985. "Management of the External Resources Gap, Profile and Structure of the Debt." In *Collected Papers on External Debt Management and Financial Technique.* New York: United Nations Centre of Transnational Corporations, August.

Gurría, José A. 1988. *La Reestructuración de la Deuda: El Caso de Mexico.* México, D.F.: Lecturas 61 de El Trimestre Economico.

Gurría, José A. 1989. "Evolución y Características de la Deuda Externa de México." Presentation before the Comisiones de Hacienda y Crédito Público y Programación y Presupuesto in the Chamber of Deputies. April.

Gurría, José A. 1993. *La Política de la Deuda Externa.* Mexico, D.F.: Fondo de Cultura Económica.

Gurria, José A., and R. Sergio Fadl. 1990. "Debt Equity Swaps. The Mexican Experience." Paper prepared for the United Nations Centre of Transnational Corporations. New York.

Gurria, José A., and R. Sergio Fadl. 1991. *Estimación de la Fuga de Capitales en México, 1970-1990.* Washington, D.C.: Inter-American Development Bank.

Reyes Heroles G.G., Jesús. 1988. "Multi-mini-menú: Elementos para avanzar en la solución del Problema de la Deuda Externa de México." Mimeo.

Reynoso, Alejandro. 1989. "Nota Técnica sobre Equivalencias entre los diferentes Esquemas del Menú Mexicano." México, D.F.: Secretaría de Hacienda y Crédito Público, mimeo.

Secretaría de Hacienda y Crédito Público. 1991. *Mexico: A New Economic Profile.* Mexico, D.F.: Secretaría de Hacienda y Crédito Público.

Van Wijnbergen, Sweder. 1990. "Mexico's external debt restructuring in 1989-1990." *World Bank Working Papers.* Washington, D.C.: The World Bank.

Villareal A., René. 1988. *Deuda Externa y Política de Ajuste: El Caso de México, 1982-1986.* México, D.F.: El Trimestre Economico.

APPENDIX 1

Table 1
Total Foreign Debt, 1973-1993
(in millions of dollars, as of December 31, each year)

Year	Public	Private	Bank	Banco de México	Total
1973	7,071	2,066	n.a.	n.a.	9,137
1974	9,975	2,224	n.a.	n.a.	12,199
1975	14,449	4,480	n.a.	n.a.	18,929
1976	19,600	6,500	n.a.	n.a.	26,100
1977	22,912	6,800	n.a.	1,200	30,912
1978	26,264	7,200	n.a.	1,200	34,664
1979	29,757	10,500	n.a.	n.a.	40,257
1980	33,813	16,900	n.a.	n.a.	50,713
1981	52,961	21,900	n.a.	n.a.	74,861
1982	58,874	19,107	7,958	240	86,179
1983	62,556	18,919	10,321	1,204	93,000
1984	69,378	17,270	6,183	2,433	95,264
1985	72,081	16,719	4,824	2,943	96,567
1986	75,351	16,061	5,551	4,028	100,991
1987	81,407	15,107	5,837	5,119	107,470
1988	81,003	7,028	8,097	4,786	100,914
1989	76,059	4,969	8,960	5,126	95,114
1990	77,770	6,135	7,759	6,508	98,172
1991	79,988	8,692	8,214	6,759	103,653
1992	75,755	11,159	6,044	5,957	98,915
1993	78,747	20,245	23,635	4,795	127,422

Source: Secretaría de Hacienda y Crédito Público.

1. The reduction of the balance of the foreign public debt in 1989 is explained by the retirement of debt that some institutions received as payment for the sale of state firms (1,830 million dollars); swaps of public debt for capital, authorized prior to November 1987 (750 million dollars); net repayments (323 million) and in the rate of exchange of the dollar with regard to other currencies (2,041 million).
2. The reduction of outstanding public debt is explained by debt repurchase operations.
3. This debt corresponds to Special Drawing Rights.

Table 2
Public Sector Foreign Debt by Source of Financing, 1977-1985
(in millions of dollars)

	1977	1978	1979	1980	1981	1982	1983	1984	1985
Total	22,912	26,264	29,757	33,813	52,961	58,874	62,556	69,378	72,080
Multilateral agencies	2,278	2,539	2,826	3,286	4,016	5,041	4,432	4,879	5,945
Bilateral	1,625	1,394	1,209	1,406	2,337	2,978	3,406	3,628	4,582
Commercial banks	19,338	22,286	25,652	29,042	46,386	5,399	50,087	56,866	57,812
Others (includes lenders)	31	45	71	79	182	5,456	4,631	4,005	3,741

Source: Secretaría de Hacienda y Crédito Público.

Table 2, cont.
Public Sector Foreign Debt by Source of Financing, 1986-1993
(in millions of dollars)

	1986	1987	1988	1989	1990	1991	1992	1993
Total	75,351	81,407	81,003	76,059	77,770	79,987	75,755	78,747
Multilateral agencies	7,411	8,126	10,470	10,099	14,685	15,187	15,645	16,241
Bilateral	5,751	8,098	8,794	8,392	11,702	12,949	12,949	15,064
Commercial banks	58,787	62,498	57,786	53,492	47,035	45,781	45,781	37,972
Others (includes lenders)	3,401	2,686	4,003	4,076	4,349	6,071	6,071	9,471

Source: Secretaría de Hacienda y Crédito Público.

Table 3
Balance of Payments, 1980-1993
(percentage of GDP)

	1980	1981	1982	1983	1984	1985	1986	1987	1988	1989	1990	1991	1992	1993
Current account	-5.5	-6.4	-3.6	3.6	2.4	0.4	-3.1	2.7	-1.5	-2.9	-2.9	-4.7	-6.9	-6.6
Income	8.4	8.4	12.9	15.5	14.4	12.4	13.5	15.7	13.2	12.6	16.8	15.1	14.0	14.6
(including maquiladoras)														
Expenditures	9.7	9.6	8.5	5.7	6.4	7.9	9.6	9.4	11.7	12.4	12.9	13.5	18.9	18.4
Interest payments	3.2	3.8	7.2	6.8	6.7	5.5	6.4	5.7	5.0	4.5	3.3	3.0	2.3	2.4
Capital account	5.9	10.5	5.7	-1.0	0.0	-1.0	1.4	-0.4	-0.8	1.5	3.4	7.1	7.9	8.7
Gross international reserves	4.0	5.0	6.8	4.9	8.1	5.8	6.8	13.7	6.6	6.9	10.3	17.5	18.6	24.5
(in billions of dollars)														
Reserves/current account income	17.9	18.0	-1.0	17.0	24.7	18.4	26.9	43.6	19.5	18.0	18.5	30.7	30.5	36.8
Net indebtedness	1.6	4.2	4.9	1.8	0.9	0.0	0.5	3.0	0.3	0.0	1.0	-0.1	-0.7	0.8
(public sector)														

Source: On the basis of information from the Secretaría de Hacienda y Crédito Público.

Table 4
Overall Results of the Two Swap Program Auctions
(millions of dollars)

	Original Value	Nominal Value	Discount Rate (%)	Amount of Rights Assigned
First auction	1,000.0	774.8	52.1	485.3
Discount bonds	666.0	440.8	26.2	325.1
Par bonds	334.0	334.0	52.1	160.2
Second auction	2,500.0	1,753.8	52.0	1,200.0
Discount bonds	2,132.5	1,386.3	26.2	1,023.7
Par bonds	367.5	367.5	52.0	176.4
Total	3,500.0	2,528.6	52.0	1,685.3
Discount bonds	2,798.5	1,827.1	26.2	1,348.8
Par bonds	701.5	701.5	52.0	336.6

Source: Secretaría de Hacienda y Crédito Público.

Table 5
Exchange of Interbank Facilities
(millions of dollars)

Debtor Bank	Interbank Liabilities as of July 2, 1991	Redemption Liabilities (weighted average)	Redemption/ Total Liabilities (%)	Discount Rate (%)	Amount of Privatization Bonds
Total	3776.4	1169.7	31.0%	1.6	1151.4
International	625.2	375.5	60.1%	0.92	372
Somex	518.8	180.9	34.9%	1.4	178.4
Bancomer	1227	400.7	32.7%	1.8	393.7
Serfin	422.9	67.4	15.9%	1.1	66.7
Comermex	523.7	78.5	15.0%	1.3	77.5
Banamex	458.8	66.7	14.5%	5.3	63.2

Source: Secretaría de Hacienda y Crédito Público.

APPENDIX 2

FOREIGN DEBT

EQUIVALENCIES AMONG THE DIFFERENT OPTIONS OF THE MEXICAN MENU

1. Equivalence between reduction of principal and reduction of interest without adjusting for risk

For the option of principal reduction, r dollars of interest are paid each year for each dollar of debt. If the debt decreases in such a way that each dollar of old debt is paid 0 centavos of new debt, then the present value of the new debt is given by the equation:

(1)
$$\Theta\left[\int_0^T re^{-rt}\,dt + e^{-rT}\right] = \Theta = VP_{(1)}$$

where:

T = Years to maturity of the new debt.

r = Market value of interest.

Θ = Dollars of new debt for dollar of old debt.

In the case of the interest reduction option, one pays only 0 (100 percent) of the original interest, in such a way that the present value is given by the equation:

(2)
$$\overline{\Theta}\left[l + e^{-rT}\right] + e^{-rT} = VP_{(2)}$$

The equivalency between the options of reduction of debt value and reduction of interest rates is given by the simultaneous solution of equations (1) and (2):

(3)
$$\overline{\Theta} = \Theta - \frac{e^{-rT}}{1 - e^{-rT}}$$

where:

$\overline{\Theta}$ = Percentage of interest continuing to be paid.

2. Equivalence between reduction of principal and reduction of interest adjusted for Mexico-risk

The concept of adjusting for Mexico-risk consists of applying the prevailing discount on the secondary market of the Mexico debt to the part of the total debt not guaranteed. In this way, in the case of the option of principal reduction with a guarantee of N years of interest and a guarantee of principal, the present value of each dollar of debt is given by the equation:

$$(4) \qquad \Theta \left[Nr + \left(1 - R\right)\left(e^{-Nr} - e^{-rT}\right) + e^{-rT} \right] = VP_{(4)}$$

where:

N = Number of years of guarantees.

$(1 - R)$ = Value of a peso of old debt in the secondary market.

R = Mexico-risk.

T = Years to maturity of the new debt.

Θ = Dollars of new debt exchanged for each dollar of old debt.

With respect to the option of reduction of interest rates, which also are guaranteed the principal and part of the interest, the present value is given by the equation:

$$(5) \qquad \overline{\Theta} \left[\overline{N}r + \left(1 - R\right)\left(e^{-\overline{N}r} - e^{-r\overline{T}}\right) \right] + e^{r\overline{T}} = VP_{(5)}$$

Equalizing equations (4) and (5) gives the following equivalency:

$$(6) \qquad \overline{\Theta} = \frac{\Theta \left[Nr + \left(1 + R\right)\left(e^{-Nr} - e^{-rT}\right) + e^{-rT} \right] - e^{r\overline{T}}}{\overline{N}r + \left(1 - R\right)\left(e^{-\overline{N}r} - e^{-r\overline{T}}\right)}$$

where:

N = Number of years of guarantees in the interest reduction option.

T = Years to maturity of the interest reduction option.

Θ = Percentage of interest continuing to be paid.

VII

BRADY PLANS FOR COMMERCIAL BANK DEBT RELIEF

Diego Aramburú

INTRODUCTION

More than five years have passed since U.S. Treasury Secretary Nicholas Brady launched in a speech what turned out to be the most popular of all debt reduction schemes proposed after the eruption of the debt crisis. Mr. Brady offered U.S. government and official multilateral support in obtaining debt and debt service relief from foreign commercial bank creditors for those countries that successfully pursued comprehensive structural adjustment programs supported by the International Monetary Fund (IMF) and the World Bank.

Through August 1994, seven countries — Argentina, Costa Rica, Mexico, Nigeria, the Philippines, Uruguay, and Venezuela — have availed themselves of this opportunity and have issued Brady bonds in exchange for their previously rescheduled bank loans with a cumulative face value of $83.7 billion. Eight more countries are expected to receive similar treatment in the next few years. In the case of Latin America, there have already been five experiences to learn from, and, in all likelihood, five more countries in the region (Dominican Republic, Brazil, Ecuador, Panama, and Peru) will be reaching an agreement and could very well benefit from the analysis of previous experiences.

The purpose of this paper is to measure the degree of success that Latin American governments have had negotiating their Brady-style agreements with commercial creditors. "Success" from the standpoint of the debtor government will be measured here as the amount of debt and debt service reduction achieved under the Brady agreement as a percentage of the debt restructured. Debt and debt service reduction are estimated by subtracting the present value of the new claim from the present value of the old debt and adjusting for prepayments made by the debtor.[1]

THE ANATOMY OF A BRADY DEBT REDUCTION

The reduction of commercial bank debt and debt service under Brady-style guidelines can be achieved through a variety of mechanisms. These include discounted cash buy-backs, discounted exchanges, asset swaps, and securitization of debt.

The universe of Brady bond debt instruments has become more diverse since Mexico concluded the first Brady agreement. The central feature of a Brady plan is the menu of options offered to the holders of existing debt. The variety of options and structures is designed to accommodate the preferences of different debt holders in a manner consistent with the funding strategy of the restructuring country.

Although the exact terms of these options vary somewhat from country to country, a considerable respect for precedent has kept the structures very similar. The Venezuelan, Philippine, and the ongoing Brazilian Brady plans have included a more complicated "menu of options," such as debt conversion bonds, front-loaded interest reduction bonds, and new money bonds. Following is the explanation of the most common options offered in a Brady agreement.

Debt Buy-Back

The basic premise of debt buy-back is that debtor countries buy their own debt at a discount, usually at a price close to that of the secondary market. According to Claessens and Diwan (1989),[2] the efficiency of such operations for the debtor depends on the implicit rate of return of using the debtor's or borrowed funds in a buy-back relative to that obtained on alternative uses of the funds — assuming that the latter would be available for uses other than debt reduction. The net effect of a debt reduction through a cash buy-back can be estimated by subtracting the actual cost of the buy-back from the nominal amount retired.

Discount Bonds

These bonds are named for the manner in which they are exchanged for loans. The debt holder receives a face amount of these bonds, which is reduced by the discount negotiated in the Brady agreement. Because of the discount, these bonds are also known as principal reduction bonds. Discount bonds typically have principal and interest guarantees[3] and bullet maturities of 25 to 30 years. Debt reduction is obtained and can be estimated directly from the discount of principal since debt service is kept at a market prevailing rate, usually LIBOR plus a spread.

Par Bonds

So named because they are exchanged dollar for dollar for existing debt, par bonds are also known as interest reduction bonds. These bonds typically have principal and interest guarantees, a fixed coupon or coupon schedule, and bullet maturities of 25 to 30 years.

Because the face amount of debt remains the same, debt relief is provided by a below-market-rate coupon. The amount of debt service reduction can be estimated from the present value of the reduction in future interest payments arising from the below market fixed interest rate path on the new instruments relative to expected future market rates. The calculation is based on the estimated term structure of interest rates at the time of agreement in principle.

Front-Loaded Interest Reduction Bonds (FLIRBs)

Front-loaded interest reduction bonds usually have fixed coupons that step up from low levels for the first few years, after which they pay a floating rate. They carry no principal collateral, and their interest collateral is released after the step-up period. These bonds have amortization schedules that give them a shorter average life (about ten years) than par or discount bonds to compensate investors for the lack of principal collateral. Debt service reduction through this option is less significant than that obtained through par bonds, and it is limited to the first few years of below-market fixed coupons.

New Money Bonds and Debt Conversion Bonds (DCBs)

New money and debt conversion bonds are generally issued together through the new money option of an exchange menu, which is designed to give debt holders an incentive to invest additional capital or "new money." For every dollar of new money bond that is purchased with cash, the investor may exchange existing debt for DCBs in a ratio negotiated in the Brady agreement (usually $4 to $6 of DCBs for every dollar of new money).

This provides an incentive to invest new money because the DCBs are usually made more attractive than the bonds available in other options. New money bonds and DCBs typically pay LIBOR plus a spread and amortization schedules that give them a ten- to fifteen-year average life. Since the DCBs pay market rates and the new money bonds are actually new debt, neither of these alternatives constitutes debt or debt service reduction.

THE LATIN AMERICAN BRADY EXPERIENCE
Mexico

On July 23, 1989, Mexico reached an agreement in principle with its Bank Advisory Committee on a term sheet (1989-1992 Financing Plan) outlining a debt and debt service reduction plan under the auspices of the Brady initiative. The agreement covered $48.23 billion in medium-term commercial bank claims ("eligible debt") on Mexico. Holders of these claims were presented with a menu of debt exchange options that included the following:

1. Exchanging loans for long-term bonds issued at face value and paying a reduced fixed interest rate (par bonds);

2. Exchanging loans for long-term bonds issued at a 35 percent discount to face value of eligible debt, but paying market rates of interest (discount bonds); and

3. Providing "new money" equivalent to 25 percent of the face amount of loans not committed to either par or discount bonds.

On February 4, 1990, Mexican officials finalized the agreement with the country's five hundred commercial bank creditors, thus becoming the first country to implement a Brady-style debt and debt service reduction plan. The final distribution of options chosen by the creditor banks was as follows: 46.5 percent opted for par bonds that amounted to $22.42 billion. At present value, that represented debt service savings in the amount of $7.13 billion compared to a same term instrument at prevailing market interest rates.

Around 42.6 percent of the debt holders chose discount bonds totaling $20.54 billion. After the 35 percent discount, the total amount of discount bonds held was $13.35 billion. That represented an immediate debt reduction of $7.19 billion.

The holders of the $5.3 billion (10.9 percent) of the remaining loans committed to new money options. Actual issuance of the Mexican Brady bonds took place on March 28, 1990.

The cost of obtaining the collateral for this debt exchange operation totaled approximately $7.12 billion: $3.40 billion for principal collateral, $3.69 billion for the rolling interest guarantees, and $24 million for guarantees on previously issued bonds (according to clauses included in the financing plan for the issue of the Brady bonds). Funding for these enhancements was provided by the IMF ($1.70 billion), the World Bank ($2.01 billion), Japan's Eximbank ($2.10 billion), and Mexican reserves ($1.30 billion). The actual amount collateralized was $60 million higher than the cost of the collateralization due to the increase in value of the U.S. Treasury bonds (decrease in yields) in the time between the purchase of these instruments and the issuance of the Brady bonds.

Thus, the total debt and debt service reduction amounted to $14.38 billion: $7.13 billion in debt service reduction from the par bonds, $7.19 billion in principal reduction from the discount bonds, and $60 million from the excess collateral of the new instruments. This figure represented 29.8 percent of the debt being restructured.

Costa Rica

After a series of difficult negotiations, Costa Rica reached an agreement in principle for a debt and debt service reduction operation in November 1989.

The agreement covered approximately $1.5 billion of commercial bank (eligible) debt.

According to the term sheet, banks were given the option of either selling their Costa Rican debt, including arrears, to Costa Rica at 16 cents per dollar of face value or exchanging it for long-term bonds at reduced interest rates. No request for new money was made, which made the agreement a form of "exit" vehicle for the commercial banks.

On May 21, 1990, the Brady-style agreement was finalized between Costa Rica and its Bank Advisory Committee when over 95 percent of the creditor banks committed to the options. The Costa Rican government bought back $991 million of its debt, which represented over two-thirds of the country's total commercial bank exposure. At 16 cents on the dollar, this represented a cost of $159 million and net savings of $832 million.

The remaining portion of the eligible debt was refinanced and packaged into two series each of principal and interest claim bonds. Foreign commercial banks that offered 60 percent or more of their holdings for the cash buy-back were offered Series A principal bonds for the balance of their claims. These bonds have a final maturity of 20 years, a grace period of ten years, and 18 months' worth of collateralized interest payments. Approximately 16 percent ($237 million) of the amount under restructure was exchanged for these bonds.

Banks that offered less than 60 percent of their holdings were allowed to exchange the balance of their claims for Series B principal bonds, which mature in 25 years and are uncollateralized as to interest. A total of $123 million (8 percent of the eligible debt) of these bonds was selected. Both series pay a fixed and below-market coupon but include a recapture clause whereby (according to a specific formula) the rate of interest on the bonds will increase if Costa Rica's GDP increases 120 percent of the 1989 level in real terms.

Based on the estimated term structure of interest rates at the time of the agreement in principle, the present value of future interest payments arising from the below-market fixed interest path on the new par bonds resulted in an estimated debt service reduction of $101 million.

Past-due interest associated with the eligible debt that was not repurchased in the buy-back was exchanged for two series of interest claims bonds. Series A was offered to those banks that offered 60 percent or more of their holdings for the cash buy-back. These are 15-year bonds paying market interest rates, 36 months of which are collateralized. Around 4.5 percent ($67 million) of the debt restructured was exchanged for this option.

Banks that offered less than 60 percent of their holdings for the cash buy-back received Series B bonds. These have similar rates of interest and maturity but were uncollateralized as to interest. Seventy-six million dollars (5 percent of eligible debt) was exchanged for this option. Since interest claim bonds were exchanged at par value and paid market interest rates, they were not a source of debt or debt service reduction.

A total of $143 million in bridge loans from Mexico and Venezuela, $9 million from multilateral sources, and $43 million of Costa Rica's own funds helped in financing this debt exchange operation. Of the $195 million, $159 million was used for the cash buy-back and $36 million to pay for the collateral.

Net savings due to debt and debt service reduction amounted to $933 million: $832 million from the cash buy-back and $101 million from the below-market coupon par bond exchange. This figure represented 62.4 percent of the debt restructured.

Venezuela

On March 20, 1990, after 14 months of intense negotiations, the Republic of Venezuela and its Bank Advisory Committee reached an agreement in principle on a debt and debt service reduction plan of the $19.7 billion of eligible debt under the auspices of the Brady initiative. This was soon followed by the release of the 1990 financing plan to all of Venezuela's 350 foreign commercial bank creditors on June 25, 1990. The menu of options included 1) exchanging eligible debt for 30-year collateralized par and discount bonds (with terms similar to the Mexican financing plan); 2) rescheduling and exchanging existing obligations with 17-year debt conversion bonds (DCBs) while purchasing (that is, providing new money for) 15-year new money bonds which would be equal to 20 percent of the principal amount of the existing obligations that were exchanged for DCBs; 3) exchanging eligible debt for 17-year front-loaded interest reduction bonds (FLIRBs) that bear a reduced fixed coupon that steps up to LIBOR + 13/16 percent over five years; and 4) exchanging eligible debt for 91-day discount notes issued by the Venezuelan Central Bank in an amount equal to 45 percent of the original face value of the debt. These notes basically replaced a potential cash buy-back option.

Execution of the program began on October 18, 1990, when banks representing 7 percent of Venezuela's total commercial bank exposure exchanged their holdings for the short-term discount notes, thus extinguishing $1.41 billion of face value of eligible debt at a cost of $635 million, constituting net savings of $776 million.

The program culminated on December 18, 1990, when the Republic of Venezuela and the Central Bank of Venezuela issued $10.24 billion of new bearer bonds and $8.7 billion of new "collateralized" bonds in exchange for the remaining $18.29 billion of eligible debt and $1.2 billion in new funds.

The breakdown of the 93 percent remaining in commitments was as follows: 32 percent DCB/new money bonds, 37 percent par bonds, 9 percent discount bonds, and 15 percent FLIRBs. The net debt service savings from the par bonds totaled $2.20 billion. The debt reduction from the discount bonds amounted to $543 million, and the debt service reduction from the FLIRBs is estimated at $488 million.

The cost of the debt reduction totaled approximately $2.58 billion: $635 million to cover buy-back costs, $1.74 billion to pay for the principal and interest guarantees, and $211 million to provide comparable collateral for bonds issued prior to 1990. Funding for these options was provided by the IMF ($880 million), the World Bank ($500 million), Japan's Eximbank ($600 million), and Venezuelan reserves ($611 million). Net from costs, the savings of the debt and debt service reduction operation reached $3.79 billion or 19.2 percent of the debt being restructured.

Uruguay

In October 1990, the Republic of Uruguay and its commercial bank creditors agreed on a term sheet outlining a debt rescheduling package covering approximately $1.6 billion in public and publicly guaranteed medium- and long-term debt (Brady Plan). This "eligible" debt, collectively referred to as MYRA debt, had been rescheduled previously on March 4, 1988.

According to the term sheet, which was made available to all 69 creditors on November 15, 1990, Uruguay offered to buy back an estimated 39 percent of its eligible debt at 56 cents per dollar of face value. Creditors were also offered two debt exchange options: 1) exchanging debt for 30-year fixed rate bonds (par bonds) with principal collateralized by U.S. Treasury zero-coupon bonds and 18 months of interest guaranteed by authorized securities or 2) rescheduling and exchanging existing obligations with 17-year debt conversion bonds (DCBs) while purchasing (that is, providing new money for) 15-year new money bonds that would be equal to 20 percent of principal amount of the existing obligations which were exchanged for DCBs. Both bonds would pay market rates of interest plus varying spreads and be uncollateralized as to principal and interest.

Creditor banks responded favorably to the options, particularly the cash buy-back, since the rate of 56 cents per dollar was higher than the secondary market price of Uruguayan debt at the time that the term sheet was finalized. Of the three options, 39 percent of the creditors committed to the buy-back, 33 percent opted for the par bonds, and 28 percent provided new money in the amount of $90 million to obtain debt conversion/new money bonds.

The total cost of the debt and debt service reduction reached $463 million: $355 million to cover the cash buy-back and $108 million to pay for the collateral. The resources were provided mostly by the multilateral organizations, including the IDB, and the country's own reserves.

As a result of this arrangement, net savings for the country totaled $425 million: $278 from the cash buy-back plus $160 million in debt service reduction through the par bonds minus $13 million due to the decrease in value in U.S. Treasury bonds bought as collateral. This figure accounts for 26.4 percent of the debt restructured.

Argentina

On April 7, 1992, the Republic of Argentina and its Bank Advisory Committee reached an agreement in principle on the settlement of the country's previously rescheduled medium- and long-term debt ("eligible debt") owed to foreign commercial bank creditors. A term sheet was issued on June 23, 1992, detailing two options available to creditors for settlement of these claims. Essentially, eligible debt could be exchanged for 30-year collateralized fixed rate par bonds and floating rate discount bonds.

On April 7, 1993, $19.29 billion of eligible debt was reportedly exchanged. Approximately two-thirds ($12.66 billion) was exchanged at face value for par bonds with the remaining 34 percent ($6.63 billion) of the stock of eligible debt exchanged at a 35 percent discount to face value (or $4.3 billion) for discount bonds. On October 29, 1993, as part of its past-due interest (PDI) agreement with creditors, Argentina issued $6.66 billion of floating rate bonds (FRBs), which represented 85 percent of the expected issuance amount.

The cost of the debt reduction package amounted to $3.06 billion, all of which was used to buy the collateral that, at the time of the debt exchange, paid for the $2.73 billion necessary to cover all guarantees. The funds were provided by the IMF, the World Bank, the IDB, Japan's Eximbank, and Argentina's own resources.

Argentina's net savings from the Brady agreement totaled $6.28 billion: $2.32 billion from the discount option exchange, $4.29 billion from the par bond debt service reduction, and a loss of $330 million from purchasing the collateral. Net savings accounted for 32.5 percent of the original amount restructured.

CONCLUSIONS

Table 1 summarizes the main findings of this study. By estimating the debt and debt service reduction as well as the cost of the selected Brady options, it is possible to measure the degree of success that Latin American governments have had in negotiating their Brady-type agreements with their commercial creditors.

The clear winner among the five countries that have already negotiated their Brady restructuring is Costa Rica. The estimated net savings from its commercial bank debt and debt service reduction operations amounts to $933 million, 62.4 percent of the original amount of debt being restructured. The

Table 1
Outcomes of Brady Plans in Latin America
(US$ millions)

	Buy-back	Discount Bond	Par Bond	Other Bonds	Collateral	Total
Mexico						
Total	0	20546	22427	5258	0	48231
Reduction*	0	7191	7130	0	7182	21503
Cost	0	0	0	0	7122	7122
Net savings	0	7191	7130	0	60	14381
Saved/total %	0.0%	35.0%	31.8%	0.0%	0.0%	29.8%
Costa Rica						
Total	991	0	360	143	0	1494
Reduction*	991	0	101	0	36	1128
Cost	159	0	0	0	36	195
Net savings	832	0	101	0	0	933
Saved/total %	84.0%	0.0%	28.1%	0.0%	0.0%	62.4%
Venezuela						
Total	1411	1769	7446	9074	0	19700
Reduction*	1411	543	2195	488	1739	6376
Cost	635	0	0	0	1950	2585
Net savings	776	543	2195	488	(211)	3791
Saved/total %	55.0%	30.7%	29.5%	5.4%	0.0%	19.2%
Uruguay						
Total	633	0	529	447	0	1609
Reduction*	633	0	160	0	95	888
Cost	355	0	0	0	108	463
Net savings	278	0	160	0	(13)	425
Saved/total %	43.9%	0.0%	30.2%	0.0%	0.0%	26.4%
Argentina						
Total	0	6627	12659	0	0	19286
Reduction*	0	2319	4290	0	2726	9335
Cost	0	0	0	0	3059	3059
Net savings	0	2319	4290	0	(333)	6276
Saved/total %	0.0%	35.0%	33.9%	0.0%	0.0%	32.5%

*Present value at time of exchange.
Sources: World Bank, IMF.

bulk of the reduction came from the buy-back operation at the highly discounted price of 16 cents per dollar of face value.

Far behind is Argentina, with a net savings over total debt restructured ratio of 32.5 percent, followed closely by Mexico with an equivalent ratio of 29.8 percent. Uruguay's net savings totaled $425 million, equivalent to 26.4 percent of the debt restructured, and Venezuela ends the list with a ratio of net savings to total debt of 19.2 percent, the worst Brady deal for a Latin American government to date.

Two questions, one technical and the other more fundamental, emerge clearly from these findings. First, why do countries offer and banks choose different alternatives? Second, and more obvious, why did some countries get better deals than others?

The offering and selection of different alternatives respond to opportunity costs of countries and creditors, respectively. Countries with ample reserves and significantly discounted debt are generally interested in buying back their debt directly or in the secondary market through a third party. This may result in overall larger savings for the country than the relief obtained through a Brady deal. Creditors are willing to accept this option if the buy-back price is at least equivalent to the market (and book) value and it reduces exposure in a country in which they have no interest.

On the other hand, countries with liquidity problems push for the discount option since it represents an immediate relief through a discounted principal and also because it requires less collateral than the par option. If, in addition, the creditor has a long-term commitment and interest in that country, the creditor does not mind selecting the discount option since it has a similar or better present value than the par or buy-back options.

No specific trend has been observed in the selection of options other than the widening of such options. The overall estimated present value of the Bradys in progress seems to be lower than that of previous experiences (higher net savings for the countries), however.

Since the countries currently undergoing negotiations toward Brady agreements have taken longer due to their economic difficulties, an hypothesis that may answer the second question is that countries with lower payment capacity benefit from higher savings in their Brady deal.

Although there are not yet enough observed experiences to establish a statistical relationship, a simple plot between debt relief and GNP per capita for the five countries under study suggests, as expected, a negative relationship (see Graph 1). However, other indicators of payment capacity such as debt and debt service to exports, GNP, or reserves do not relate clearly to debt relief.

A more comprehensive analysis of Latin American governments' success in reducing their external debts should include the restructuring of their bilateral

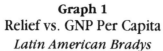

Graph 1
Relief vs. GNP Per Capita
Latin American Bradys

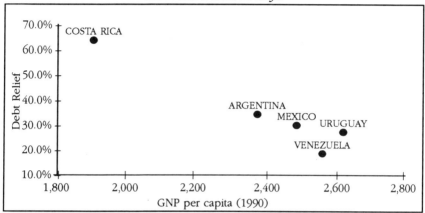

and multilateral obligations as well as the coversion of their debt into equity. In this last case, however, valuation may prove difficult if not impossible.

The group of middle-income Latin American countries that still has to come to terms with bank creditors on debt reduction packages is now half of the initial number. Moreover, all of these remaining countries — Brazil, Dominican Republic, Ecuador, Panama, and Peru — have already begun negotiations with the banks.

Even if these countries implement good policies, in the absence of debt restructuring, many face difficult external prospects. It is important that debt restructuring result in a stream of debt service obligations that the country can meet while also achieving the satisfactory growth performance necessary to sustain the momentum of sound policies. For many of these countries, achieving this objective will require debt reduction on terms going beyond those obtained in recently completed packages, consistent with the lower price of their debt on the secondary market.

A particular problem faced by the countries now negotiating with banks is the high proportion of interest arrears and trade-related credits that in earlier packages received privileged treatment. In packages completed thus far, interest arrears have normally been either cleared or rescheduled rather than made eligible for debt reduction, while trade-related debt has been excluded altogether from the restructuring packages.

This treatment has reflected valid concerns about avoiding moral hazard and preserving access to trade financing. Nevertheless, for some of the remaining countries, adaptation in this area may be unavoidable if lasting solutions to their debt problems are to be found.

NOTES

1.   The methodology is described in detail in Annex I of Charles Collyns, and others, 1992, *Private Market Financing for Developing Countries,* World Economic and Financial Surveys. Washington, D.C.: International Monetary Fund.

2.   Claessens, Stijn, and Ishac Diwan. 1989. "Market-Based Debt Reduction." In *Dealing with the Debt Crisis,* eds. Ishart Husain and Ishac Diwan. Washington, D.C.: The World Bank.

3.   Usually U.S. Treasury 30-year zero-coupon bonds to collateralize the principal of the bonds, while two or three semiannual interest payments are guaranteed by securities of at least double A credit quality.

VIII

GOVERNMENT CREDITWORTHINESS

Robert Grosse

ABSTRACT

This study uses secondary data on the external debt of Latin American countries and indicators of economic policy and macroeconomic conditions to model the success of the countries in becoming more creditworthy in the 1990s. The intent is to measure greater success as increased international creditworthiness and also to consider alternative indicators of success — such as increased secondary market debt price and increased probability of repayment of outstanding external debt — which were not available in earlier periods.

The most striking finding in this analysis is that the key external macroeconomic factors such as the level of international interest rates and the growth rate of the industrial countries have had the greatest impact on countries' international creditworthiness during 1986-1993. In addition, some government macroeconomic policies have had a significant impact on their creditworthiness. Most notably, the government's ability to generate long-term debt inflows has alleviated foreign exchange shortages and contributed positively to improvements in creditworthiness. The fiscal deficit was significantly negatively correlated with creditworthiness in one model, while monetary policy was insignificant, though correctly signed in both models.

INTRODUCTION

The external debt crisis that swept Latin America during the 1980s was accompanied by sharp economic downturns in most of the countries of the region from 1982 onward. Through a combination of economic growth in the industrial countries, lowering of dollar interest rates, and sound economic policies in the debtor countries, the crisis has been overcome. In fact, the 1990s have shown Latin America to be a leading target of international investment and economic growth. How has this "economic miracle" taken place?

Beyond any doubt, the private sector solutions to the debt crisis that were proposed and followed by lending banks, multinational companies, and other private sector actors in Latin American finance played a major role in defusing the crisis. Debt-equity swaps, debt buy-backs, and even the underlying operation of the secondary market in government external debt were instrumental in resolving the impasse of nonpayment by the sovereign borrowers from their private foreign commercial bank creditors. The Brady Plan (1989) defined by the U.S. Treasury Department affirmed these initiatives and provided U.S. government backing to some of the debt conversion instruments. These phenomena have been analyzed in detail in other studies (e.g., Grosse 1992; Dornbusch, Makin, and Zlowe 1989; Cohen 1991).

By 1994, the borrowing governments have achieved generally improved positions on debt indicators such as debt/GDP and interest/export ratios, as well as higher levels of per capita income and faster economic growth rates than in the 1980s. Despite the similarity of Latin American countries in improving economic conditions and dealing with external debt, there are many quite important differences in policies, achievements, and circumstances.

This paper explores these differences in the context of external debt. It looks at the degrees of success or failure of ten countries in improving their international creditworthiness. The fundamental research question is what factors have had the greatest influence on improving country creditworthiness since the debt crisis. The approach is principally econometric; that is, country performance is compared on a statistical basis to demonstrate the factors that have contributed to improved creditworthiness. Conclusions are then drawn based on the factors that contribute most importantly to restoring country creditworthiness in international financial markets.

METHODOLOGY

This study uses secondary data on the external debt of Latin American countries and indicators of economic policy and macroeconomic conditions to model the success of the countries in becoming more creditworthy in the 1990s. Similar measures were used by Dhonte (1975) and Feder and Just (1977) in studying country credit risk in the 1970s and by Cohen (1991) and Tang and Espinal (1989) in the 1980s. The intent is to measure greater success as increased international creditworthiness and also to consider alternative indicators of success — such as increased secondary market debt price and increased probability of repayment of outstanding external debt — which were not available in earlier periods.

The direct measure of increased creditworthiness would be an indicator such as the credit rating given to a sovereign borrower by a rating agency such as Moody's or Standard and Poor's. Such ratings are available for a few of the countries in Latin America, but only for specific security issues such as eurobonds. The empirical problem in using this indicator is that eurobond issues only restarted for Latin American sovereign issuers in 1991, so there is a very short time period available for consideration. Only the governments of Argentina, Mexico, and Venezuela issued eurobonds during 1991-1993,[1] so the range of countries is quite limited. The ratings are also only for these issues, so that updates typically do not take place, and thus only one observation exists for most issues.

A second measure of creditworthiness is the credit terms offered to sovereign borrowers in renegotiation of foreign loans. These terms (especially interest rate and maturity) accompany the jumbo loan packages for each of the countries in the sample. Presumably, a lower interest rate and a longer maturity indicate greater confidence in the borrower and, thus, greater success in our context. A problem with this measure is again the lack of much history on the loan packages. Most were renegotiated in the late 1980s, and most were renegotiated before that only once or twice, so that statistical analysis of the measure is difficult.

A third measure of creditworthiness is the probability of repayment of sovereign loans to commercial bank lenders. While new securities issues may be evaluated directly for creditworthiness, as noted above, the number of such issues is small. In contrast, most of the governments in Latin America have restructured their external commercial bank debt during the crisis period, so a history of valuations and risk measures exists on these debts. An effort to specify and calculate the probability of sovereign loan repayment was undertaken by Grosse and Rodriguez (1994) for ten countries on the most recent jumbo loan package as reported by the World Bank (see Table 5). It uses a bond valuation model that incorporates world interest rates, secondary market prices, and loan maturities and grace periods. The repayment probability produced by the model is an ex ante measure of the risk, rather than one based on historical data alone. The Grosse and Rodriguez measure is a probability calculated on a monthly basis, so it offers greater statistical flexibility than the previous measures. This model is presented in the Appendix to the paper.

And finally, the degree of creditworthiness of a sovereign borrower may be measured by the proxy — secondary market loan price — which is an observed value that reflects the government's likelihood of meeting future loan servicing commitments on the foreign commercial bank debt that is traded in the secondary market. A sense of the improved creditworthiness of governments in Latin America can be gained from inspection of secondary market prices during the past seven years, as shown in Table 1.

Notice that the positions of Chile and Mexico have improved dramatically since 1986, while Ecuador and Peru remain quite weak, although improved in the early 1990s. Argentina experienced hyperinflation and deep recession in the

Table 1
Prices of Latin American Loans
(loan sale price relative to face value)

Country	July 1985	July 1986	July 1987	July 1988	July 1989	Aug 1990	Aug 1991	July 1992	July 1993
Argentina	60-65%	63-67%	46-49%	24-26%	18%	14%	38%	50%	54%
Brazil	75-81%	73-76%	58-61%	51-52%	34%	38%	24%	33%	63%*
Chile	65-69%	64-67%	68-70%	60-61%	64%	70%	89%	91%	93%
Colombia	81-83%	80-82%	81-83%	65-67%	62%	63%	79%	88%	n.r.
Ecuador	65-70%	63-66%	45-47%	25-27%	17%	16%	24%	35%	33%
Mexico	80-82%	56-59%	55-57%	51-52%	44%	40%	59%	68%	74%
Peru	45-50%	18-23%	10-12%	5-6%	5%	5%	13%	17%	34%
Venezuela	83-85%	75-78%	70-72%	54-55%	41%	46%	68%	64%	68%

* Brazil issued a large quantity of "new money" bonds in 1991. The quotes here are for par bonds issued earlier during renegotiations in the mid-1980s. Both are quoted in today's secondary market.

Sources: Shearson Lehman Brothers International, Inc., for 1985-1988; *LatinFinance*, various issues, for 1989-1993.

late 1980s, then dramatic recovery in the early 1990s. Both of these conditions are reflected in the secondary market prices. Brazil's situation is not clear from the table. Original par bonds trade today for less than two-thirds of face value, while new money bonds trade for over 80 percent of face value — thus, interpretation of the Brazilian values must be cautiously done, as below.

MODELS

Tests of improved creditworthiness are carried out using two of the measures above: secondary market loan prices and probabilities of loan repayment. Both dependent variables are explained with a set of macroeconomic and policy variables. The independent variables reflect, first, the governments' abilities to achieve stable and sustainable monetary and fiscal policies; second, their abilities to produce favorable macroeconomic conditions in the country; and third, their abilities to deal successfully with foreign creditors. A fourth influence is expected from external conditions, principally the lending and aggregate demand conditions in the industrial countries which so heavily affect the Latin American borrowers. The four groups of factors are shown together in equation (1).

(1)

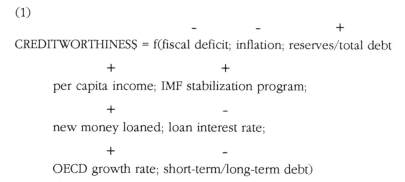

The signs above each variable denote the expected sign of the relationship with international creditworthiness. The four groups are discussed next.

Government Policy Variables

The *fiscal deficit* measures a government's need to generate funding to balance government spending with tax and other revenues. A greater fiscal deficit requires greater financing, from both domestic and foreign sources. In addition, a greater fiscal deficit may indicate a government's inability to control spending, which makes that government a riskier debtor. Thus, a larger fiscal deficit is expected to produce a lower creditworthiness.

Inflation is an indicator of domestic policy and macroeconomic instability. Greater inflation implies less ability of a government to finance its fiscal needs with taxes or other revenues and more need to print money. Higher inflation, as with large fiscal deficits, may indicate the government's inability to control the domestic economy and, thus, presents a possibility of lower creditworthiness.

Domestic Macroeconomic Indicators

The *reserves/total debt ratio* measures directly the country's ability to produce adequate foreign exchange earnings (through exports, incoming investment, and so forth) to cover debt servicing. An alternative measure of debt servicing would be interest payments to exports, which was used in another specification of the model. The greater the amount of debt or the lower the export earnings (or foreign exchange reserves), the lower the creditworthiness of the government as an international borrower.

Another measure of domestic economic stability is *per capita income*. In this case, the greater the per capita income, presumably the greater will be the country's ability to generate savings that could be mobilized to service foreign debt. One would expect that higher per capita income would be associated with better creditworthiness.

Success in Dealing with External Creditors

Additionally, government policy may be measured as the degree of success achieved in dealing with foreign lenders, private and official. Indicators on this issue include the amount of sovereign debt conversion into local equity or bonds, the ratio of short-term to long-term debt structure, successful negotiation of an IMF stabilization plan, and new money loaned by commercial bank creditors.

Conversion of debt from commercial bank loans into long-term bonds, or into local equity investment, or into other instruments eliminates the converted debt from future loan servicing needs. Obviously, conversion into bonds would not necessarily produce a change in debt servicing, but the conversions all have included reduced debt burdens by cutting interest payments, or extending maturities, or reducing principal values. The use of conversion programs implies a flexibility on the government's part, which may be indicative of a move to open up the economy to more market-based financial instruments and practices (e.g., debt-equity swaps). It may be viewed as an indicator of the governments' willingness to meet debt servicing obligations, separate from the ability to do so. In sum, greater conversion of debt into reduced-service bonds or into equity is expected to result in greater creditworthiness of the government.[2]

Since longer-term credit generally provides a greater assurance of funding over time than short-term debt, the longer the average credit terms, the better the repayment probability. That is, the less frequently the borrower has to resort to the international financial markets for new loans, the less risky the borrower will appear. This idea was measured as the ratio of short-term to long-term external debt of the country. The lower the *ratio of short-term to long-term debt*, the higher the expected creditworthiness of the country.

Commercial bank decisions to extend new credit to sovereign borrowers are another indicator of increased creditworthiness of the borrowers. This increased credit is difficult to separate out from increased lending that results from postponing and capitalizing interest payments that have not been made. Truly "voluntary" new lending is quite difficult to measure. Despite this caveat, *net transfers of funds by foreign commercial banks* will be used as an explanatory variable. Greater net transfers of funds to the borrowing country (i.e., extension of new credit) is expected to imply greater creditworthiness.

The existence of an *IMF stabilization program* during the 1980s tended to imply that the government had been unable to deal successfully with its foreign debt, and thus, it needed to seek out this "lender of last resort." Countries that resorted to IMF stabilization and funding earlier tended to have worse international financial problems. On this basis, greater creditworthiness should be associated with later negotiation of an IMF stabilization program and even more with the ability to avoid such a program.[3]

External Economic Conditions

Although not under the control of the debtor governments, changes in international borrowing costs will affect their abilities to service the debt. Most important, changes in *dollar lending rates* will affect debt servicing, with higher rates implying greater difficulty in making payments. The most common base for loan contracts is the London Interbank Offered Rate, LIBOR, which is combined with a spread to give loan interest costs. Since most countries in the region have experienced very similar spreads over LIBOR,[4] the same rate is applied to all countries. It thus functions as a shift variable in the model, affecting all governments' loan servicing abilities equally.

Additionally, the ability of foreign importers to absorb the debtor's exports may enable greater debt servicing capability. For this reason, the *growth rate of the OECD countries* is included as a measure of the rest of the world's demand for borrower country exports.

Data on the dependent variables were available on a monthly basis, but some of the independent variables were only available on an annual basis. To avoid serious statistical problems and to obtain a reasonably large sample size, linear quarterly interpolations were made on annual data; the monthly data were aggregated for quarters, and the regressions were run on quarterly values.

TEST RESULTS

Table 2 presents results of statistical modeling to explain country creditworthiness based on the variables discussed above. High correlations between some independent variables made a few of the results difficult to interpret.[5] The models shown in Table 2 include the total set of variables.

Table 2
Regression Results — Country Creditworthiness

Dependent Variable	Secondary Market Price	Repayment Probability
Constant	114.84 (12.73)**	110.34 (29.12)**
Reserves/total debt	45.67 (2.65)**	-0.31 (-0.01)
Budget deficit	-0.001 (-0.71)	-0.001 (-7.06)**
Short-term/long-term debt	-165.62 (-6.77)**	-23.38 (-2.55)**
Inflation	-1.04 (-1.12)	-0.21 (0.72)
Per capita income	-0.001 (-2.11)*	0.001 (0.52)
New money loaned	-0.006 (-1.01)	-0.009 (-4.46)**
IMF stability program	-4.69 (-2.24)*	-0.12 (-0.12)
Interest rate	-6.67 (-8.02)**	-1.80 (-4.66)**
OECD growth rate	2.02 (2.65)*	0.61 (2.14)*

* Significant at 0.05% level.
** Significant at 0.01% level.

Number of observations	195	116
R^2	0.63	0.58

The model of creditworthiness using secondary market prices as shown in the first column gives strong support to the hypothesized relationships between macroeconomic variables and creditworthiness and some support to the hypothesized relationships between the policy variables and creditworthiness. Most variables, except the government budget deficit, inflation, and new lending, are significant at the .05 level, and most are significant at the .01 level. All of the variables, except for the existence of an IMF stabilization program and per capita income, have the expected signs; per capita income is negatively associated with secondary market prices,[6] as is the existence of an IMF program.

Using probability of loan repayment as our measure of creditworthiness led to results as shown in the second column of Table 2. In this case, per capita income, existence of an IMF stabilization plan, inflation, and reserves/external debt were insignificant, but the rest of the factors produced significant coefficients and the expected signs. The explanatory power of this model was approximately the same as for the previous version; about two-thirds of the variation in creditworthiness was explained by the economic factors.

The models in Table 2 were estimated as random effects models (Greene 1992) to account for differences in the relationships across countries. Both the error components specification and the least squares, dummy variable specification were tried, and the former produced a better model based on the Hausmann test statistic. Slight autocorrelation was present among the error terms, so a Prais-Winsten transformation was performed. The results shown in the table are for this generalized least squares model.

INTERPRETATION OF RESULTS

The findings above tell quite an interesting story about the impacts of government policies and macroeconomic conditions on the creditworthiness of sovereign borrowers in Latin America in the early 1990s. The most significant impact on creditworthiness came from *international interest rates*, proxied by LIBOR. The externally determined cost of funds was the most significant factor contributing to increases in secondary market prices and probabilities of loan repayment. Latin American governments had no control over this rate, but their abilities to service foreign debt improved strikingly due to lower dollar interest rates as the debt crisis diminished.

The second measure of external factors affecting creditworthiness, the *OECD countries' growth rate*, proved to be highly significant and positively correlated as well. This measure supports the idea that the industrial countries' abilities to purchase Latin American exports (and possibly, the industrial countries' financial capability to extend more credit) do indeed improve the Latin American countries' perceived creditworthiness. Thus, both of the variables that are outside of Latin American governments' control proved quite important in determining their creditworthiness.

The *ratio of short-term to long-term debt* was strongly negatively correlated with the two creditworthiness measures. This implies that the government's ability to obtain long-term rather than short-term funding plays a major role in improving repayment capability. This stands to reason, since long-term borrowing assures the debtor of funds availability for a longer period of time without need to refinance. Also, fees are paid less often when the loans are not renewed as frequently. In sum, the greater the portion of total debt that is long term, the better the creditworthiness of the country.

Continuing in descending order of significance of the variables, the *ratio of official reserves to external debt* contributed to explaining the changes in country creditworthiness during the period. This positive relationship may be interpreted as showing that sound economic policy stimulated capital inflows due to increased investor confidence in the country. It also may be related to the large trade surpluses produced by many of the countries as a result of severe economic downturns and, thus, reduced demand for imports.[7]

Net funds transfers from foreign commercial bank lenders were highly negatively correlated with increased creditworthiness. This is probably due to the "forced lending" problem that caused banks to extend additional credit to sovereign borrowers to cover unpaid interest and principal, rather than voluntary lending that would imply greater confidence in the borrowers. Due to accounting and regulatory rules, it was easier for U.S. banks to show loan nonpayment as an increase in principal (and future interest due) rather than to record loans as being nonperforming. This led banks to capitalize interest nonpayments, i.e., to list new lending to the borrowers rather than to show losses. The forced nature of the lending is corroborated by the lending growth rate, which was over 20 percent per year to Latin American countries during 1974-1982, but then dropped to less than 5 percent per year during the debt crisis.

The existence of a *stabilization program with the International Monetary Fund* had a negative influence on creditworthiness, consistent with the hypothesis. This may be interpreted as a negative signal that only non-creditworthy borrowers should need to resort to such a program. Alternatively, it may mean that the earlier the country had to turn to the IMF for financial assistance, the worse its credit position. Since the variable was specified as a 0,1 dummy, the countries with longer-standing IMF programs in place showed lower creditworthiness rankings. Thus, existence of an IMF stabilization program indicated a worse credit risk.

The two measures of government policy showed only fair performance in the modeling. The *government budget deficit* was, as expected, negatively correlated with creditworthiness. The deficit was only significant in the repayment probability model, though it was the dominant variable in that model. This result generally supports the reasoning that greater budget deficits imply lower confidence by international lenders in the government's debt management capability and directly imply greater financing needs.

Inflation, an indicator of the government's ability to control domestic monetary conditions, had the expected negative relationship to creditworthiness. However, in both models, the relationship was insignificant. This finding gives only weak support for the notion that monetary policy and, particularly, control of inflation contribute to improved creditworthiness.

Finally, the level of *per capita income* was negatively correlated with creditworthiness in one model and insignificant in the other. This finding mildly contradicts the hypothesized relationship, which held that greater incomes would lead to better creditworthiness.

INDIVIDUAL COUNTRY EXPERIENCES

It is instructive to examine individual countries in somewhat greater detail to interpret the above results. For one thing, although policy variables appear to be important contributors to creditworthiness, there have been quite varied policies followed by the ten governments in the sample. Also, even with all of the efforts to reduce the debt burden via debt-equity swaps, buy-backs, bond issues, and other means, the total debt still has not fallen. Table 3 gives some idea of this situation.

Table 3
External Debt Features of Selected Latin American Countries

	Total Debt 1987 (billions $)	Total Debt 1992 (billions $)	Debt/Exports 1987->1992 (percent)	Net FIN Transfers 1987->1992 (billions $)
Argentina	58.5	67.6	695->454	-2.6-> 1.8
Brazil	123.8	121.1	431->310	-7.5-> 3.3
Chile	21.5	19.4	331->149	-0.6->-0.5
Colombia	17.0	17.2	222->162	-1.7->-2.3
Costa Rica	4.7	4.0	316->150	0.1-> 0.0
Ecuador	10.5	12.3	424->339	0.1->-0.5
Mexico	109.5	113.4	364->243	-1.5-> 2.6
Panama	5.6	6.5	98->223	-0.2->-0.3
Peru	17.5	20.3	478->453	0.2-> 0.2
Venezuela	34.6	37.2	268->220	-4.3->-0.3

Source: World Bank, *World Debt Tables 1993-1994.*

In all cases, the country has been able to reduce the debt/export ratio, almost always quite dramatically. In most cases, the country has reduced or reversed the net outflow of commercial bank funds from 1987 to 1992, with the exceptions of Colombia and Panama. But, in almost all cases, the level of total debt has increased over that five-year period, with the exceptions of Brazil, Chile, and Costa Rica. Next, consider the very different experiences of two countries in some more detail.

Argentina and Brazil were both hit with severe recessions, hyperinflation, and unserviceable levels of external debt during the 1980s' crisis. Argentina's government, beginning in 1990, was able to establish a new policy regime and to achieve a high degree of economic stability with high real growth. Brazil's government has not been able to escape severe hyperinflation (more than 1000 percent per year) by 1994, though real growth has been positive in the 1990s. The two different government policy responses and country experiences during the same time period shed more light on the issue of regaining international creditworthiness.

Argentina

Argentina has carried out possibly the most successful stabilization program in Latin America during the early 1990s. This country went from more than 1000 percent annual inflation in 1990 to less than 10 percent annual inflation in 1993. The government budget deficit was cut from 5.7 percent of GDP in 1987 to 0.3 percent of GDP in 1992. A Brady Plan debt restructuring in 1992 produced a significant reduction in total sovereign external debt. The government was even able to return to international capital markets via eurobond issue beginning in 1993.

These macroeconomic policies were accompanied by a massive plan of privatization of state-owned firms, from the national telephone company to the national oil company. Labor legislation was revised to eliminate major barriers to employment flexibility. Limits on foreign participation in the economy and on operation of financial markets were eliminated.[8] In sum, the Argentine business and economic environment was drastically opened since 1990, and the foreign sovereign debt situation improved along with the general macroeconomy.

Secondary market debt prices rose from less than 20 percent of face value in 1990 to more than 60 percent in 1993. The loan repayment probability for Argentina's main restructured sovereign debt package likewise rose from an estimated 15 percent in 1990 to over 80 percent in 1993. It appears that the success in stabilizing fiscal policy is consistent with the model's implications and that the success in stabilizing monetary policy has contributed as well to general economic recovery (though not significantly contributing to improved creditworthiness in the model).

The original model was rerun separately for Argentina and Brazil, as shown in Table 4.

Table 4
Regression Results — Individual Country Creditworthiness

Country	Argentina	Brazil
Constant	223.96	—
	(2.52)**	
Reserves/total debt	1058.8	2057.6
	(2.23)**	(2.41)**
Budget deficit	.001	-.001
	(0.87)	(-0.19)
Short-term/long-term debt	294.25	-949.17
	(0.28)	(-5.27)***
Inflation	-1.21	0.43
	(-1.14)	(0.11)
Per capita income	-.001	7.12
	(-1.93)*	(2.25)**
New money loaned	.503	.057
	(2.52)**	(4.54)***
IMF stability program	1.17	-1.74
	(0.27)	(-0.22)
Interest	-6.79	-0.94
	(-1.16)	(-0.18)
OECD growth rate	68.46	7.38
	(3.34)***	(2.01)**

* Significant at .10% level.
** Significant at .05% level.
*** Significant at .01% level.

Number of observations	20	19
R^2	0.87	0.91

Both models use secondary market price as the dependent variable.

The model was run as an ordinary least squares regression, with no country dummy variables and no need for correction of autocorrelation.[9] The results for Argentina show that the most significant contributing factors to improved creditworthiness were the growth rate of the OECD countries (+), along with the ratio of official reserves to external debt (+), the level of per capita income (-), and the amount of new lending (+). These results are similar to those in the full model, except that the amount of new lending has positively affected Argentina's creditworthiness, as contrasted with the ten-country model, where the relationship was negative.

Brazil

Brazil has achieved much less success than many other Latin American countries in rebounding from the debt crisis period. Inflation remains at more than 2000 percent per year in 1994, while the fiscal deficit was cut to 14 percent of GDP in 1990 from 21.5 percent of GDP in 1988. The macroeconomy has been growing in the early 1990s at a positive rate, but stability has not yet been achieved.

The external sovereign debt has improved in the secondary market, with the price rising from a low of 24 percent of face value in 1991 to more than 60 percent of face value in 1993. Similarly, the probability of repayment of the largest debt package has improved from a low of 60 percent in 1990 to a high of almost 90 percent in 1993. It appears that the improvement in external conditions (loan interest rates and industrial-country growth) has contributed to Brazil's debt servicing capability sufficiently to produce these major improvements in creditworthiness, despite the lack of government policy success, especially in monetary affairs. Brazil has been able to obtain a better short-term to long-term debt profile than Argentina, with 83 percent of its external debt in long maturities, versus 76 percent for Argentina.

Applying the model of country creditworthiness to Brazil produced the results in Table 4. As with Argentina, the OECD growth rate strongly positively related to Brazil's creditworthiness. In addition, the ratio of short-term to long-term debt (-) was strongly negatively associated with improvements in Brazil's position, as in the full ten-country model. Other significant variables included the ratio of reserves to external debt (+) and per capita income (+). The amount of new lending (+) was positively correlated with Brazil's creditworthiness, as with Argentina but different from the full ten-country model. Apparently, for these two large countries, new lending was indeed voluntary rather than forced during the period under study.

These results of the individual country models broadly conform to the ten-country results. The insignificance of the interest rate term is a notable difference, though the sign of this variable was negative as expected in both cases. The individual country results should be viewed with some reservation, due to the small number of observations available for analysis.

The comparison of two quite distinct policy responses to the external debt problem shows that, despite divergent results in controlling inflation and government spending, Argentina and Brazil have achieved similar improvements in creditworthiness. This result is probably due to the dominance of industrial-country conditions (viz., lower interest rates and higher growth rates) on the credit market. In contrasting the two countries, Argentina's monetary and fiscal policies have been more successfully stabilized, while Brazil has achieved a higher percentage of long-term external financing. These two results seem to have canceled in terms of their impacts on country creditworthiness.

CONCLUSIONS

The most striking finding in this analysis is that the key external macroeconomic factors — the level of international interest rates and the growth rate of the industrial countries — have had the greatest impact on Latin American countries' international creditworthiness during 1986-1993. In addition, some government macroeconomic policies have had a significant impact on the countries' creditworthiness. Most notably, the government's ability to generate long-term debt inflows has alleviated foreign exchange shortages and contributed positively to improvements in creditworthiness. This is not a simple relationship, however, since the government may achieve this result by opening up the financial system to freer funds flows, or it may impose import restrictions and export subsidies to improve the trade balance, or it may change domestic policy management to raise investor confidence and thus reverse the capital flight of earlier years.

Additionally, the ability of the government to improve its fiscal balance has appeared important as an influence on loan repayment probabilities. This emphasizes the importance of fiscal policy more than monetary policy as a leading contributor to improved creditworthiness.

Overall, the non-policy variables appear to dominate the policy ones in this analysis. This should not be surprising, because the foreign lenders are more interested in the country's overall ability to meet debt servicing needs, rather than just the government's.

Undoubtedly, Latin American governments have not escaped the problem of very large foreign debt. The crisis has been reduced to being a problem, but one which is being managed successfully in most cases. The return of Latin American governments to international capital markets, especially the eurobond market, testifies to this fact. This study demonstrates that governments need to pay most attention to the term structure of their debt and to their fiscal policies as the keys to increased creditworthiness. It also shows that global economic conditions largely drive the borrowing abilities of Latin American countries; both dollar lending rates (-) and industrial-country growth rates (+) strongly influence country creditworthiness.

Table 5
Loan Package Characteristics

Country	Date of Issue	Jumbo Loan Face Value	Maturity	Annual Interest Rate	Grace Period
Argentina	Aug 1987	$25.3 billion	2006	LIBOR + 13/16	8 years
Bolivia	July 1987	$22 million	2012	9.25 fixed	none
Brazil	Nov 1988	$61.0 billion	2007	LIBOR + 13/16	7 years
Chile	June 1987	$2.9 billion	2002	LIBOR + 1	5 years
Colombia	n.a.	none	—	—	—
Costa Rica	Nov 1989	$225 million	2009	6.25 fixed	10 years
Ecuador	Nov 1987	$631 million	1997	LIBOR + 1	3 years
Mexico	Aug 1987	$7.1 billion	2017	LIBOR + 13/16	7 years
Nicaragua	Apr 1989	$1.26 billion	2009	LIBOR + 3/8	3 years
Panama	Oct 1985	—	1997	LIBOR + 1.375	19 years
Peru	May 1983	—	1991	LIBOR + 2.25	none
Venezuela	Sept 1988	$20.3 billion	2001	LIBOR + 7/8	none

Sources: International Financial Corporation, *International Capital Markets*. Washington, D.C.: World Bank, 1990; *LatinFinance*, various issues.

NOTES

1. Government-owned companies issued eurobonds in Brazil, Chile, and a few other countries during this period, but direct government issues were limited to the three countries listed.

2. Unfortunately, in the statistical modeling, the debt conversion variable was highly correlated with four of the other independent variables and produced highly significant results. It was eliminated from the modeling process.

3. Alternatively, existence of an IMF stabilization program may demonstrate that a government has achieved a viable stage of economic policy management and that future policies can be expected to follow orthodox lines (budget deficit reduction, restraint on printing money, opening of financial markets and trade, and so on). Thus, greater creditworthiness should be associated with successful negotiation of an IMF stabilization program. As with the new lending variable discussed below, the negative interpretation of an IMF stablization program was hypothesized, based on discussions with lenders during the period.

4. See, for example, the descriptions of new loan characteristics in the monthly magazine *LatinFinance.*

5. In particular, the variables reserves/external debt, short-term/long-term debt, and OECD growth rate were intercorrelated with coefficients of about .7 in each pairing. The variables were maintained in the regressions presented because their economic meanings are quite different. The resulting regression thus may be inefficient, though not biased.

6. This may be due to the dominance of a particular country such as Brazil — in fact, a least squares, dummy variable model accounting for each country produced a highly insignificant coefficient for per capita income.

7. The reserves/total debt ratio was not significant in the final GLS model of loan repayment probability as shown in Table 2. It was significant in the simple least squares model and signed as expected.

8. See, for example, Business International Corporation, 1993, *Investing, Licensing, and Trading Conditions,* Argentina section. New York: Business International.

9. The Durbin-Watson statistics in both individual country models were approximately 2.2, indicating no need to transform the error terms for autocorrelation.

References

Boehmer, E., and W. Megginson. 1990. "Determinants of Secondary Market Prices for Developing Country Syndicated Loans," *Journal of Finance* 45:1517-1540.

Cline, William. 1983. *International Debt and the Stability of the World Economy.* Washington, D.C.: Institute for International Economics.

Cohen, Daniel. 1991. *Private Lending to Sovereign States.* Cambridge, Mass.: MIT Press.

Dhonte, Pierre. 1975. "Describing External Debt Situations," *IMF Staff Papers,* No. 1, 159-186.

Dornbusch, R., J. Makin, and D. Zlowe, eds. 1989. *Alternative Solutions to Developing Country Debt Problems.* Washington, D.C.: American Enterprise Institute.

Eaton, J., M. Gersovitz, and J. Stiglitz. 1986. "The Pure Theory of Country Risk," *European Economic Review* 30(3):481-513.

Feder, G., and R. Just. 1977. "A Study of Debt Servicing Capacity Applying Logit Analysis," *Journal of Development Economics* July, 25-39.

Greene, William. 1992. *LIMDEP Version 6.0.* Bellport, N.Y.: Econometric Software, Inc.

Grosse, Robert, ed. 1992. *Private Sector Solutions to the Latin American Debt Problem.* Coral Gables, Fla.: University of Miami North-South Center.

Grosse, Robert, and Ricardo Rodriguez. 1994. "Probability of Repayment for Latin American Loan Packages," *Agenda Paper #8,* University of Miami North-South Center.

Tang, J.C.S., and C.G. Espinal. 1989. "A Model to Assess Country Risk," *Omega* 17(4): 363-367.

Appendix 1

Data Sources

Debt: value of total external debt, as well as short-term and long-term debt, from public and private sources, as presented in *World Debt Tables*. Washington, D.C.: World Bank, various issues.

Reserves: official reserves as registered with the International Monetary Fund and listed in line 1l.d of *International Financial Statistics*.

New Money: net transfers from foreign commercial bank lenders as presented in *World Debt Tables*. Washington, D.C.: World Bank, various issues.

Income = GNP/population: GNP from line 99a; population from line 99z in *International Financial Statistics*. Washington, D.C.: International Monetary Fund, various issues.

Inflation: percentage change in consumer price index, line 64 in *International Financial Statistics*.

Interest Rate: London Interbank Offered Rate as listed in International Interest Rates table of *International Financial Statistics*.

Balance of Payments: trade balance as presented in line 77acd of *International Financial Statistics*.

Fiscal Deficit: taken from *Economic and Social Progress in Latin America*. Washington, D.C.: Inter-American Development Bank, various issues.

Country Risk: inflation as measured in line 64 of *International Financial Statistics*. Also measured for the recent period as the country risk index published in *Euromoney* magazine in every September issue and by *Institutional Investor* magazine.

IMF Stabilization Program: a binary variable based on existence or not of an IMF stabilization program (i.e., stand-by arrangement, extended arrangement, structural adjustment arrangement, enhanced structural adjustment arrangement) as reported in *International Financial Statistics*.

OECD Growth Rate: GDP growth rate for OECD countries as reported in line 99b.r of *International Financial Statistics*.

Secondary Market Prices for foreign debt of Latin American countries were published from 1986 to 1993 by *LatinFinance* magazine on a monthly basis.

Appendix 2

Bond Valuation Model
Applied to Latin American Sovereign Debt

The model assumes that investors are risk-neutral and that the tax environment for loans is as follows:

1. Interest payments (C) are taxable as ordinary income.

2. Capital gains are subject to the capital gains tax rate (G) and are paid when the loan matures at time t = m, if the issuing country does not default on the loans.

3. If the issuing country defaults on the loan, no principal payment is made, and the owner of the loan is entitled to an immediate deduction of the full purchase price of the loan (B) at the capital gains tax rate.

As a result of these assumptions, a loan selling at a discount, and with a face value of F dollars at maturity, m, provides an after-tax cash flow at time t = 1,...,m with the following distribution:

(1)
$$CF(t) = C(1-T) + I(t)\left[F(1-G) + BG\right] ; \text{ with probability } p^t$$
$$= BG ; \text{ with probability } p^{t-1}(1-p)$$

where I(t) is an indicator function defined by I(t) = 0 for t = 1,...,(m-1) and I(m) = 1.

Under the risk-neutrality assumption of the model, the price of a risky loan, B, equals the sum of the discounted expected cash flows, where the discount rate is the default-free, tax-free rate, i. This means that the current price of the loan must be equal to:

(2)
$$B = \sum_{t-1}^{m} \frac{E\left[CF(t)\right]}{(1+i)^t}$$

Using Equation (1) to calculate the expected cash flow, E[CF(t)], substituting in Equation (2), and simplifying gives the valuation expression used to calculate the probability of repayment:

(3)

$$\left[C\left(1-T\right)+BG\frac{1-p}{p}\right]\left[\sum_{t-1}^{m}\left(\frac{p}{1+i}\right)^{r}\right]+\left[F\left(1-G\right)+BG\right]\left(\frac{p}{1+i}\right)^{m}-B=0$$

With the exception of the probability of repayment, p, all of the parameters in this implicit equation are publicly available, so the probability of repayment can be readily found from Equation (3) through trial and error.

Equation (3) is the fundamental relationship linking the various loan parameters, including the probability of repayment, p, with external economic parameters such as the risk-free rate, i. However, before the model can be used empirically to extract the probability of repayment for Latin American debt packages, it must be adjusted to reflect the actual behavior of the loans. For example, many of the jumbo loans carry adjustable rates of interest, usually expressed as the LIBOR rate plus a fixed spread. When a rate adjustment is made, the interest payments remain fixed for the next 3, 6, or 12 months, depending on the loan, after which time the rate is adjusted using the LIBOR rate prevailing then. As a result, only the next few contractual interest payments are known with certainty at any given time. Since all future interest payments, C, must be considered in Equation (3), we assume that the current LIBOR rate will prevail from the time of the next adjustment until maturity. This naive "no change" model for forecasting interest rates generally outperforms experts' forecasts and other more sophisticated econometric techniques, as shown by Elliot and Baier (1979) and Woolford (1991).

It is also necessary to adjust Equation (3) so that it reflects the fact that most Latin American loans have principal amortization provisions before maturity. Typically, the loan enjoys a grace period before the amortization process begins. After that time, the principal is amortized linearly until maturity. While these loan characteristics do not affect the basic interpretation of the valuation model, they make the actual empirical equation used to find the probability of payment much more cumbersome.

To illustrate how the basic valuation expression, Equation (3), must be adjusted, consider an adjustable rate loan that matures m months from now, has a grace period that ends in g months, and that requires an interest rate adjustment A months from now. When the loan's interest rate was adjusted a few months ago, it was set at $[(C_0/F) \times 100]$ percent per month. Based on our discussion, this means that from $t = 1$ to $t = A$, the monthly interest payment on the loan will be $\$C_0$ and that it is expected to be $\$C_1$ from $t = (A + 1)$ to

$t = g$. Notice, however, that because the principal will be linearly amortized from $t = g + 1$ to $t = m$, the contractual interest payment is expected to be less than $\$C_1$ over that period, since the interest payment will also decrease linearly as the loan balance outstanding is reduced. Under this scenario, the following expression is required to obtain the probability of repayment, p:

(4)

$$\left[C_0\left(1 - T\right) + BG\frac{1-p}{p} \right] \left[\sum_{t-1}^{A} \left(\frac{p}{1+i}\right)^r \right]$$

$$+ \left[C_1\left(1 - T\right) + BG\frac{1-p}{p} \right] \left[\sum_{t=A-1}^{A} \left(\frac{p}{1+i}\right)^r \right]$$

$$+ \left[\frac{F\left(1 - G\right) + BG}{m - g} \right] \left[\sum_{t=g-1}^{m} \left(\frac{p}{1+i}\right)^r \right]$$

$$+ \left[C1\left(1 - T\right) + BG\frac{1-p}{p} \right] \left[\sum_{t=g-1}^{m} \left(\frac{m-t+1}{m-g}\right)\left(\frac{p}{1+i}\right)^r \right] - B = 0$$

The first term of Equation (4) represents the present value of the $\$C_0$ payments which are known with certainty until the next interest rate adjustment is made at $t = A$. It also includes the present value of the tax deduction, BG, that arises in case the loan defaults. The second term has a similar interpretation, but it pertains to the uncertain cash flows from $t = A + 1$ to $t = g$, which are expected to be $\$C_1$. The third term represents the after-tax principal cash flows, which the loan's owner will collect from the time just after the grace period ends until maturity, assuming the loan does not default. The final term represents the value of the linearly decreasing interest payments, as well as the value of the tax deduction in case the loan defaults between the grace period and maturity.

CONCLUSIONS AND A LOOK AHEAD

Robert Grosse

The previous chapters have consistently demonstrated the severity of the debt crisis in Latin America during the 1980s and the governments' strong responses to it. The analyses have just as clearly demonstrated the lack of a single recipe for responding to the varied costs and problems that accompanied the external debt crisis in different countries. The Bolivian solution would not have served in Argentina or Mexico — the lending banks would not have been able to suffer the direct losses that were incurred in the debt repurchase agreements with Bolivia if the size of the debt had been much larger. The Brazilian lack of a solution was not followed elsewhere, and perhaps the smaller countries would have encountered excessively costly barriers to such a non-solution due to reprisals from the lenders. Of the Big 3 Latin American countries, Mexico was most closely tied to the United States and was most quickly forced to adjust to the debt crisis. All of these examples illustrate the kinds of considerations that made government responses to the debt crisis differ widely across the region.

It is also clear that the government responses were not always *government solutions* to the external debt problem. This is true for two distinct reasons. First and foremost, the external debt was never viewed as *the* problem, but rather as a symptom of problems in obtaining foreign financial resources, in generating confidence on the parts of both foreign and domestic investors, and in achieving a stable path of economic development. Therefore, governments pursued the primary problems directly and only dealt with the debt as part of a total economic policy package. And second, whether or not a government pursued policies toward ameliorating the debt overhang, external conditions in industrial-country economies and in international credit markets had a major impact on the debt situation. Faster economic growth in the industrial countries, as well as lower dollar interest rates in the United States and in the euromarkets, contributed to solving the Latin American external debt problem regardless of government policies.

The debt crisis was spawned by a period in the 1970s when Latin America's principal commodities were experiencing rapid price increases, and, hence, most countries in the region experienced improved terms of trade. At the same time, dollar interest rates were relatively low, so that servicing of dollar loans was very low cost in real terms. These conditions combined in the mid-1970s with a downturn in industrial-country economies, thus making Latin American borrowers appear quite attractive in international markets.

The increased lending that did occur in the 1970s was brought to an abrupt halt in 1982, with the Mexican government's declaration of its inability to meet external debt servicing requirements. Mexico, as most other countries in the region, was faced at that time with reduced international prices on key exports (in this case, oil) and increased borrowing costs, due to the historically very high U.S. dollar interest rates that peaked in 1981. As other countries encountered the same conditions, their governments made the same statements about inability to service foreign debt, and the crisis was under way. This story has been told widely and often (e.g., Kuczynski 1987; Grosse 1992).

By the end of the 1980s, through creative strategies defined by private sector participants in the financial markets, instruments such as debt-equity swaps, debt buy-backs, debt sales and swaps in the secondary market, and others were being used to manage the debt problem. Banks from most lending countries had chosen to write down debt values on their books and sometimes to sell the loans at large discounts. At the same time, governments in Latin America were frequently offering opportunities to redeem their impaired foreign bank loans via swaps for local equity investments (sometimes as partial payment for buying shares during privatizations of state-owned companies). Flexibility on both sides produced a series of steps forward that eliminated the impasse in debt negotiations and that paved the way toward renewed creditworthiness for many Latin American borrowers.

A happy confluence of circumstances in the early 1990s added more positive impetus to the Latin American recovery. Dollar interest rates fell to historic lows in the early part of the decade, even as Europe and Japan were suffering through protracted recessions. Once again, Latin American borrowers became more attractive due to their rapidly growing economies and, perhaps, due to the economic opening that permitted foreign investors to enter the market more actively. Traditional loan demand was weak because of the recessions in major parts of the industrial world, so the door began to open again to Latin American borrowers.

The story is not completely rosy, of course. Latin American government borrowers today face major barriers to borrowing in international capital markets, as some of their debt remains impaired and traded at a discount in the secondary market. Latin American private sector borrowers, and state-owned enterprises with healthy financial statements, are finding increasing access to foreign bank loans, foreign bond sales, and even equity issues via mechanisms such as the American Depositary Receipt. The net result is that foreign finance is playing a growing role in supporting economic development in Latin America, but most of it is not being channeled through government hands.

This should not be a surprising outcome, given the global shift toward deregulation, privatization, and general support for free markets in the late 1980s and early 1990s. The key questions today are not about government external debt, but about generating savings for economic development. Latin American countries have broadly achieved positive and relatively rapid growth rates during the past five years. This result has been accomplished through a combination of better macroeconomic policies, a reduction in borrowing costs in international markets, and a general increase in confidence on the part of investors from abroad and from the region itself.

The necessary steps from here are to build economic infrastructure and continue sound economic policies in the years ahead. These steps will help to build the rate of domestic savings and attract foreign savings to Latin America. The processes of selling off state-owned enterprises seem to be generating both cash for government needs and improved performance of the privatized firms (Ramamurti 1994). The development of local securities markets is moving ahead, often driven by share issues in the processes of privatization (International Finance Corporation 1994). The elimination of tariff and non-tariff barriers to trade in the region are adding to the confidence of business in general and investors in particular, so that both the trade itself and capital investment to produce tradable goods are growing rapidly. All of these pieces contribute to the climate of confidence in the economies of Latin American countries that continues to attract domestic and foreign investors.

Obviously, cyclical economic downturns will occur in the not-distant future. Perhaps not so obviously, with no alternative model such as communism, nor even a reasonable hope to mount a successful military dictatorship (because of fierce opposition by the world economic community and particularly by the United States), it is most likely that economic swings will be managed in Latin America through economic policy instruments, fiscal and monetary, rather than other means. This reality is repeatedly reinforced as more and more economic integration agreements bind the countries of the Western Hemisphere together more tightly.

Both external and internal debt will continue to cause problems for governments that are seeking to build up the economic and social infrastructures of their countries. The problems that one may anticipate in looking forward to the year 2000 are principally those of how to compete for the financial resources against local private sector borrowers and foreign borrowers. That is, the governments in Latin America need to compete increasingly in local financial markets against private sector issuers of debt and equity instruments, in contrast to the past when government issues dominated all the Latin American securities exchanges. They also have to compete in international financial markets against not only local private sector issuers but also private and public borrowers from the rest of the world. These conditions are rapidly becoming a reality and will be so long before the year 2000.

Government responses to the external debt crisis of the 1980s, coupled with private sector responses and fortuitous conditions in the international economy, have eliminated the crisis. The problem surely has not gone away permanently — Latin American countries have suffered severe debt crises with fair regularity, approximately every fifty years, since their independence in the 1820s (Marichal 1989). What we can expect is a shift in critical concerns for the rest of this decade away from foreign debt toward mobilizing savings, maintaining stable growth paths, and dealing with inevitable business cycles.

REFERENCES

Grosse, Robert, ed. 1992. *Private Sector Solutions to the Latin American Debt Problem.* Coral Gables, Fla.: University of Miami North-South Center.

International Finance Corporation. 1994. *Emerging Stockmarkets Factbook.* Washington, D.C.: IFC.

Kuczynski, Pedro-Pablo. 1987. "The Outlook for Latin American Debt," *Foreign Affairs* (Fall):129-149.

Marichal, Carlos. 1989. *Century of Debt Crises in Latin America.* Princeton, N.J.: Princeton University Press.

Ramamurti, Ravi, ed. *Privatization of Infrastructure in Latin America.* Baltimore, Md.: Johns Hopkins University Press.

INDEX

PRODUCTION NOTES

This book was printed on 60 lb. Glatfelter Supple Opaque Natural text stock with a 10 point C1S cover stock, film laminated.

The text was set in Garamond for the North-South Center Press, using Aldus PageMaker 5.0, on a Macintosh Centris 650 computer. It was designed and formatted by Stephanie True Moss, who also created the index.

The cover was created by Mary M. Mapes using Adobe Illustrator 5.5 to create the illustration and exported to Quark XPress 3.3 for the composition and color separation.

The book was edited by Jayne M. Weisblatt.

It was printed by Thomson-Shore, Inc. of Dexter, Michigan, U.S.A.